JACK BILLMEIR
MERCHANT SHIPOWNER

JACK BILLMEIR
MERCHANT SHIPOWNER

by

P. M. HEATON

THE STARLING PRESS LTD
PRINTERS & PUBLISHERS
RISCA   NEWPORT   GWENT
1989

ISBN 0 9507714 9 X

Published by P. M. Heaton, Abergavenny, Gwent, NP7 5PR

Printed by the Starling Press Ltd., Risca, Newport, Gwent, NP1 6YB

AUTHOR

Paul Michael Heaton was born at New Inn, Pontypool, in 1944 and was educated at Greenlawn Junior School in New Inn and the Wern Secondary School at Sebastopol. At fifteen he left school and commenced employment, at first in a local store and then with a builders' merchant. A year later he was appointed as a Deck Cadet in the Merchant Navy, with the Lamport and Holt Line of Liverpool, and served in their vessels *Chatham, Constable* and *Romney* usually in the Brazil and River Plate trades. He joined the Monmouthshire Constabulary (now Gwent) in 1963 and has served at Abergavenny, Cwmbran, Newport, the Traffic Department and as the Force Public Relations Officer, and now holds the rank of Inspector.

He has always maintained an interest in maritime history, and since 1977 has had numerous articles published in the magazine *Sea Breezes*. He has had the following books published:

Reardon Smith 1905-1980

The Redbrook: A Deep-Sea Tramp

The Usk Ships

The Abbey Line

Reardon Smith Line

The South American Saint Line

Welsh Blockade Runners in the Spanish Civil War

Lamport & Holt

Tatems of Cardiff

Booth Line

The Baron Glanely of St. Fagans and W. J. Tatem Ltd. (with H. S. Appleyard)

Kaye, Son & Co. Ltd. (with K. O'Donoghue)

ACKNOWLEDGEMENTS

I would like to thank all those who have helped in the compilation of this volume, particularly:—

Mr. F. W. Jones, Cardiff, and his brother the late Mr. H. S. Jones.

Mr. David Burrell, Muirkirk.

Mr. E. N. Taylor, Gosport.

Mr. Laurence Dunn, Gravesend.

Mr. Tom Rayner, Ryde, Isle of Wight.

Mr. John Clarkson, Preston.

Mr. A. Duncan, Gravesend.

Mr. K. O'Donoghue, Gravesend.

Mr. H. S. Appleyard, Sunderland.

Mr. John Lingwood, Sunderland.

Mr. B. Lawley, Manchester.

Mr. C. J. M. Carter, Wirral.

The World Ship Society Central Record Team.

Skyfotos Ltd., New Romney, Kent.

The National Museum of Wales—Welsh Industrial and Maritime Museum, Cardiff.

Cardiff Central, Newport, Cwmbran and Abergavenny Reference Libraries.

BIBLIOGRAPHY

Daily Mail 1936-1939

Echegaray, R. G.—La Marina Mercante y el Trafico Maritimo en la Guerra Civil (Libreria Editorial San Martin).

Francis, H.—Miners Against Fascism (Lawrence and Wishart, 1984).

Heaton, P. M.—The Abbey Line (Author, 1983).

Heaton, P. M.—Welsh Blockade Runners in the Spanish Civil War (Author, 1985).

Jackson, G.—A Concise History of the Spanish Civil War (Thomas and Hudson, 1974).

Jones, F. W.—Personal Recollections.

Jones, H. S.—Personal Recollections.

Lennox Kerr, J.—Touching the Adventures (George G. Harrap, 1953).

Lloyd's List for 1936-1939.

Lloyd's Register of Shipping for the period.

Lloyd's Weekly Casualty Reports 1936-1939.

Sea Breezes, July 1948.

Thomas, H.—The Spanish Civil War (Eyre and Spottiswoode, 1961).

Times 1936-1939.

Western Mail 1936-1939.

CONTENTS

LIST OF ILLUSTRATIONS

30. The tanker "Stanmore" (7) was two years old when bought in 1947. *(Tom Rayner)*.
31. The "Stanmore" (7). *(A. Duncan)*.
32. The tanker "Stanwell" (2) joined the fleet in 1947. *(Skyfotos Ltd.)*.
33. The "Stanwell" (2) in ballast. *(Skyfotos Ltd.)*
34. The tanker "Stanwell". *(Welsh Industrial & Maritime Museum)*.
35. The war-built "Stanway" of 2,902 gross tons was acquired in 1948. *(Welsh Industrial & Maritime Museum)*.
36. The "Stanfirth" was bought in 1948 from the Admiralty and converted for commercial service. *(A. Duncan)*.
37. The "Stanfirth" was a unit of the fleet from 1948 until 1961. *(Tom Rayner)*.
38. The 9,136 gross ton "Stanroyal" was acquired in 1948. She had been built in Germany in 1929. *(A. Duncan)*.
39. The "Stanroyal". *(Tom Rayner)*.
40. The "Stanburn" (3) was built in 1951 by the Burntisland Shipbuilding Co. Ltd. *(A Duncan)*.
41. The "Stanburn" (3) was sold to Russia in 1954. *(Tom Rayner)*.
42. The "Westford" of 1941 joined the fleet of Duff, Herbert & Mitchell Ltd. in 1954. She is shown under her earlier name of "Paris City". *(Tom Rayner)*.
43. The Tanker "Westbrook" built in 1942 was bought in 1955. *(Skyfotos Ltd.)*
44. The "Elstead" was acquired in 1955 and placed in the ownership of J. A. Billmeir & Co. Ltd. *(Skyfotos Ltd.)*.
45. The "Elstead" was built in 1943. *(A Duncan)*.
46. The "Stanland" of 1942 was bought from W. H. Seager & Co. Ltd., Cardiff in 1955. *(Welsh Industrial & Maritime Museum)*.
47. The "Stanfield" was bought in 1955 and converted from a tanker into an ore carrier. *(Skyfotos Ltd.)*.
48. The tanker "Stanloch" was bought in 1955. *(Skyfotos Ltd.)*.
49. The "Stanthorpe" (3) was acquired in 1955. *(Skyfotos Ltd.)*
50. The "Stancrown" was built in 1956 by J. Crown & Sons Ltd., Sunderland. *(Tom Rayner)*.
51. The "Stancrown" of 1956. *(A. Duncan)*.
52. The "Stanwear" was built in 1956 by W. Pickersgill & Sons Ltd., Sunderland. *(A. Duncan)*.
53. The "Stanwear" of 1956. *(Skyfotos Ltd.)*.
54. The "Westbay" was acquired by Duff, Herbert & Mitchell Ltd. in 1957 and sold in 1962. *(Skyfotos Ltd.)*.
55. The tanker "Stanvale" was built in Sweden in 1957 and sold later that same year. *(A. Duncan)*.
56. The tanker "Stancloud" (12,700 gross tons) was built at Newcastle by Swan Hunter & Wigham Richardson Ltd. in 1958. She was the largest and last ship to join the fleet. *(A. Duncan)*.

1. INTRODUCTION

My interest in shipping stems from spending most of my early holidays at Barry in South Wales where I used to wander around the docks. Whilst there I saw two ships which were owned by Duff, Herbert and Mitchell Ltd., the tanker *Westbrook* and the cargo tramp *Westbay*. This was a company which was owned and managed by Jack Albert Billmeir. When I started at the Wern Secondary School my first geography book was devoted to the voyages of the steamer *Stancleeve* and contained details of her voyages, cargoes carried and countries visited. I was absolutely fascinated. The *Stancleeve* started her voyage, in the book, leaving Barry with a cargo of coal for the River Plate, and I later discovered that this vessel was owned by the Stanhope Steamship Co. Ltd., of London, which was another company owned and managed by Billmeir.

Having researched and written a number of articles and books, I kept hearing about the legendary figure Jack Albert Billmeir, who had attempted to enter shipowning a number of times in the 1920s and early 1930s, and whose ventures had failed every time. However, in 1934 he formed the Stanhope Steamship Co. Ltd and bought two coasters. Success was assured for him when during the Spanish Civil War he owned over twenty ships carrying cargo to and from the territory held by the Republican side. In addition he acted as cargo broker for many other owners so trading. His ships were subjected to a considerable number of attacks by General Franco's Nationalist forces, and many were damaged, others were captured or sunk, but he continued supplying them right up to the end of the conflict. The last ship to leave Spain before the fall of the Republicans was a Billmeir ship carrying refugees. He was also involved in supplying the Chinese during their conflict with the Japanese before the Second World War. Having made a considerable fortune he invested in building new ships, and acquired many more which were relatively modern. His fleet suffered more than most during the Second World War, and again during this conflict his blockade running experience was put to good use when the Admiralty asked him to attempt to get a ship with much needed supplies through to Malta. A number of ships were sunk in this attempt, but he did succeed in getting one through to the island. In the post war period he operated up to eighteen ships, comprising tramp steamers, ore carriers and tankers, and again made large sums when he sold tonnage at times when the freight market peaked, such as during the Korean war. He was not a man to operate ships at a loss if this could be avoided, and as a result when he died on December 22, 1963, at 63 years of age, the fleet comprised of only three ships, all of which were well maintained modern units.

I have started by giving an outline of Billmeir's early career, followed by details of his entry into shipowning, and thereafter covered the Spanish Civil War in as much detail as possible, giving details of every attack known to have been made on his ships. The Second World War is covered giving details of the grievous losses suffered by the company's ships and personnel, and the story is brought up to 1964 when it was sold following his death.

I hope that readers will be as fascinated by the subject as much as I have been.

P. M. Heaton.
February, 1989.

2. JACK ALBERT BILLMEIR

Jack Albert Billmeir, the son of Joseph and Rosa Billmeir, was born on September 1, 1900 at London. He was educated at St. Marylebone School, leaving before his fourteenth birthday to take up employment in a shipbroker's office in the City of London, where he was to gain that early training which was to be of such great use to him throughout his subsequent career in shipowning.

In 1921 he married Annie Margaret Gibbs who provided a full measure of support and encouragement throughout his life. Their union, however, was childless.

Billmeir had always had plans to make a success of his life and to this end right from the start of his working life he set about accumulating some capital. Not only did he work in the City during the day, but in the evenings and at weekends he did everything in his power to earn extra cash. In this way, he turned his hand to a variety of things, selling bricks and sand, appearing on stage at a music hall, and with his wife opened a restaurant.

Having saved the princely sum of £250 he invested this in a part interest in a ship. This venture was to be a failure as was the purchase of a steam trawler in 1922, and a part interest in an 8,000 gross ton tramp steamer in 1924. In 1927 he became a member of the Baltic Exchange, but this coincided with a further disappointment followed by another failed shipping venture in 1928.

In 1931 he formed a management company, J. A. Billmeir and Co. Ltd., with offices at London. Success was actually to follow in 1934 when he formed the shipowning company, the Stanhope Steamship Co. Ltd. and prudently invested in two small coasters. With these vessels he offered to carry cargo right to the door of his customers, as it were. He specialised in carrying the unusual, and cargo which bigger operators had passed by.

It was in this way that he was to make his reputation and his fortune. Billmeir will, however, always be remembered for his involvement in the trade to Republican Spain during the Spanish Civil War, where as I will show, he operated at times in excess of twenty ships in running the Nationalist blockade.

As his reputation became established so did his standing in the industry. He became a Member of the Council of the Chamber of Shipping from 1948, and was the Chairman of the Intermediate Section from 1948-1953; Member of Shipowners' Advisory Panel of Lighthouse Commissioners 1946-1957; Apart from being a member of the Baltic Exchange from 1927, he was also a Director from 1953-58; He became an underwriting member of Lloyd's in 1932; He was Prime Warden, Shipwrights' Company

1962-63; Was honoured with an Hon. M.A. at Oxford in 1958, and was created a CBE in 1953.

He was a member of the Reform Club, the International Sportsmen's Club, Royal London Yacht Club, and was Commodore of the Royal Southampton Yacht Club. He was a keen golfer.

He had homes at —"Westbrook", Elstead, Surrey; Melfort, Argyll; Tillmouth Park, Northumberland; and Parnham, Dorset.

When he died on December 22, 1963 he was regarded as being one of the most successful shipowners to have been produced in the inter-war period. He was well regarded, but was known as a man who got what he wanted.

3. THE ENTRY INTO SHIPOWNING

Having tried to establish himself as a shipowner on more than one occasion Jack Albert Billmeir realised that to make a success of such a venture he would have to think of an idea which would guarantee him cargo in what was still a period of decline and depression. Thus he decided to operate small coasters wherever he could obtain freight, and made a particular point of offering to carry cargo right to the consignee. By choosing small vessels this would ensure that small parcels of cargo would be viable. Whilst the original vessels were to be seen carrying timber from Russia and wine from Spain, to mention but two of the trades, he undertook to deliver on many occasions right up-river, and to out of the way destinations not normally served by shipping.

The initial two ships that he bought for this purpose were steam coasters which had originally been built for Dutch owners. The two vessels were acquired from the Tyne-Tees Steam Shipping Co. Ltd., of Newcastle, and were registered in the ownership of the newly formed Stanhope Steamship Co. Ltd in 1934 and placed under the management of J. A. Billmeir and Co. Ltd. The vessels were the 505 gross ton *Sandhill* which dated from 1920 which was appropriately renamed *Stanhope,* and the *Wooler* (700 gross tons) which had been built in 1918, and was renamed in Billmeir's fleet as the *Stanmore.* Both ships had had a succession of previous owners.

The two ships proved highly successful in service, and Billmeir was well pleased with this, as it turned out, his final attempt to enter the shipping industry as an owner.

After trading the two ships for two years in the coastal and intermediate trades, he started to acquire additional ships. In all five vessels joined the relatively new fleet during 1936, of which one was to be resold almost immediately to other owners. These ships comprised the 516 gross ton coaster *Skinningrove* which dated from 1895 and was appropriately renamed *Stangrove;* the 1,236 gross ton *Eider* of 1900 which became the *Stanhill;* the 790 gross ton Latvian coaster *Alburn* which dated from 1904 and joined the fleet as the *Stancor;* the *Stanholme* (ex *Goleta*) was the largest of the vessels acquired, being of 2,473 gross tons she was a typical three island intermediate tramp steamer of the period, and dated from 1927 when completed by the Burntisland Shipbuilding Co. Ltd.

The fifth vessel was the twenty-four year old *Kenwood* which was acquired by the management company itself, J. A. Billmeir and Co. Ltd. This ship of 1,374 gross tons was sold within months to Panamanian flag owners, and she had an interesting career thereafter as in 1938 she was captured by the Nationalists during the Spanish Civil War, confiscated, and placed under the Spanish flag where she remained until broken up in 1960.

4. EXPANSION

Whilst Billmeir's entry into shipowning through the Stanhope Steamship Co. Ltd was proving to be a success, he was nonetheless hampered to some extent by his lack of capital. The period was a difficult one, and his ships were trading at a profit by his shear flair for ship management. He was a clever, astute individual and was quick to seize opportunities when they presented themselves.

Soon after the outbreak of the Spanish Civil War on July 18, 1936 he realised that there was a real opportunity to make good returns by carrying cargo into Republican held ports, when many others were reluctant to get involved. He had no such qualms, and his involvement was to grow rapidly. Not only was he prepared to send his own ships, but he acted as cargo broker for many more. It can safely be said that of all the characters to emerge as a result of the war in Spain, Jack Albert Billmeir was one of the cleverest.

The problem in Spain was that the lawfully elected Republican Government was opposed by the military and fascists who set about overthrowing the government. War broke out and the insurgents under General Franco quickly took control of half of the territory. Franco after a short while was able to control the sea lanes into Spain, and the Republican Goverment having to continue trading with the outside world, had to pay well above the normal frieght rates to shipowners prepared to run the blockade. In the early stages of the war this was not too great a problem, but as Franco's hold became tighter, less and less owners were prepared to run the risk. As a result freight rates rocketed.

It quickly became apparent that shipowners running the blockade were able to make bigger profits when using older ships which had a small capital value. Such vessels were not hampered by high war risks insurance. However, the crews of ships engaged in the trade to Spain were paid a war bonus when in the zone of hostilities.

As a result of his involvement, Billmeir bought twenty-one ships during 1937. Of these a number were quickly resold, having in some cases only undertaken one voyage to Spain. Of these ships, their average age was twenty-five years, and many had obviously seen better days.

Of the six ships in the Stanhope fleet at the start of 1937, three were disposed of during that year. The pioneer vessels *Stanhope* (1) and *Stanmore* (1) were sold, the former going to Gillie, Blair and Company of Newcastle. She had a number of owners subsequently, and was broken up in 1954 at Grays, Essex. The *Stanmore* passed to John S. Monks Ltd., of Liverpool, for whom she traded until September 1951 when handed over to shipbreakers at Preston. The other disposal was the *Stanhill* (1) which went to Greek owners, and passed to the Italian flag the following year. She was a casualty of the Second World War, being bombed by Allied aircraft at Genoa on May 12, 1944.

Sadly the smallest of the ships acquired in 1937, the seventeen year old *Stancrest* was to mark the company's first loss, as having left London on February 27, of that year, with a cargo of cement destined for Bridgwater she was posted missing with all hands.

Four of the ships bought were sold that same year to G. M. Mavroleon of Greece. These were the *Stancroft* (1,407 gross tons) of 1908, *Stanbrook* (1,383 gross tons) of 1909, *Stancourt* (1) (950 gross tons) of 1907 and the *Stanmore* (3) (1,387 gross tons) of 1919. Of these vessels the *Stanbrook* returned to the Billmeir fleet later that same year, whilst the *Stancroft* was bought back a year later. The *Stancourt,* survived under the Greek flag until June 1, 1940 when she was shelled and sunk by the German submarine *U37* 120 miles West of Cape Finisterre while on passage from Alexandria to the River Tyne. The *Stanmore* (3) had a long career under various flags, being broken up in Italy in 1968.

Two of the ships bought in 1937 were quickly resold to French owners. These were the *Stanmore* (2) (3,222 gross tons) dating from 1920 and the *Sheaf Spear* (3,050 gross tons) of 1919, which entered the fleet without change of name. The former vessel was a casualty of the Second World War, being torpedoed and sunk by HMS *Tigress* West of Cap Ferrat on February 19, 1941, whilst the *Sheaf Spear* was bombed and sunk by Allied aircraft at Palermo on March 22, 1943 whilst flying the Italian flag.

An interesting ship acquired was the French steamer *St. Pierre* of 2,456 gross tons which dated from 1908. She entered the Stanhope fleet as the *Standale* but on her maiden voyage for the company from Antwerp to Carthagena her cargo of grain shifted when 60 miles North of Leixoes, and as a result she was abandoned by her crew with a heavy list, and subsequently sank on April 3, 1937.

Other cargo ships which entered the fleet during 1937 were the *Stanhope* (2) (2,337 gross tons) which had been built in 1919, the *Stanleigh* (1,802 gross tons) of 1912, the *Stanray* (880 gross tons) which dated from 1904, the larger *Stanthorpe* (4,524 gross tons) of 1915, *Stanwold* (1,019 gross tons) of 1909, *Stanwood* (4,158 gross tons) of 1915, *Stanrock* (1,105 gross tons) of 1910, *Stancliffe* (1) of 1914, *Stangate* (1,289 gross tons) of 1912 and the *Stanforth* (1,817 gross tons) dating from 1915.

In addition, due to the demand by the Republicans for petroleum and petroleum products, Billmeir purchased three tankers during the year. These were the *Stanbridge* (5,863 gross tons) of 1917, the *Stanmount* (4,468 gross tons) of 1914 and the elderly and smaller *Stanfield* (1) of 2,432 gross tons which had been built in 1892.

An interesting transaction which took place concerned the 790 gross tons steamer *Stancor* which had been purchased in 1936 from Latvian owners, namely V. Zatorskis of Riga. In 1937 this ship was sold back to these Latvian owners and managed on their behalf by J. A. Billmeir and Co. Ltd. However during 1938 she was bought back by Billmeir and re-registered under the British flag.

This was a considerable fleet of ships. Bearing in mind that Billmeir had very little capital, it was little wonder that some of the vessels were resold after the one voyage to Spain. In a number of instances a ship would load a cargo in the United Kingdom or continent and deliver it to Southern Spain, and thereafter ballast to Marseilles where the crew would be paid off and repatriated, and the ship delivered to her new owner. One of the unusual features of the Spanish Civil War trade was that the shipowner was normally paid in advance for the voyage. Normal practise on a single voyage basis is for the shipowner to receive his payment when the cargo has arrived at its destination and been unloaded, whereas in this trade the owner was paid when the cargo had been loaded at the point of departure.

The high freight rates enabled Billmeir to increase his fleet rapidly, and in addition he received considerable sums for the brokerage of other vessels engaged in the trade.

The 1930s were difficult years, and it was a great help to British Seamen to have such a rapidly expanding fleet, as the employment provided by the Stanhope Steamship Co. Ltd was considerable. Many of these crews were signed on in South Wales or the North East coast. Billmeir built up a considerable pool of manpower and many masters and officers were to remain with him for years, and were to witness first hand his rise as a shipowner.

21

5. THE SPANISH CIVIL WAR—1937

Although the Spanish Civil War broke out on July 18, 1936, no Billmeir ship came to note in the first eight months of the war. Franco's Nationalist Navy had taken control of the Straits of Gibraltar and were patrolling the sea lanes leading to Republican held territory. They were stopping and inspecting Merchantmen around the Spanish coastline. A number of vessels had been confiscated and others had been damaged by shelling. It was a sad fact that some ships had been sunk by the Nationalists and merchant seamen were being killed.

By March, 1937 Franco had taken a considerable proportion of the Spanish mainland. Republican territory at this time actually comprised the strip of land in Northern Spain, the Basque region, from Aviles in the West to Bilbao in the East. In the South Republican territory stretched from Almeria to the French border near Port Bou. The plainlands to the North of Almeria as far as Madrid were still held by the Republicans and Franco had failed to take the capital Madrid.

Having failed in his attempt to take Madrid, Franco had set out to take the North and gradually as the months passed in 1937 he took more and more territory.

A number of incidents occurred involving British merchant ships in the early part of 1937, when Nationalist warships had stopped them, or ordered them to stop on the high seas off Spain, for the purpose of inspecting their papers and cargoes to ensure that war materials were not getting through to the Republicans. When British ships were loading in various parts of the world, Franco's agents kept a watchful eye to report any vessel suspected of loading armaments for the Republicans. '

In March, 1937 the *Stanholme* was loading at Casablanca, North Africa, for Spain, and the Nationalists made a formal complaint to the British Authorities at Gibraltar to the effect that she was indeed loading war contraband. The British Consul at Casablanca made an immediate investigation, and satisfied himself that the charge was unfounded. However, the Nationalists were not satisfied with this, and intercepted the *Stanholme* outside territorial waters and escorted her to Gibraltar, where the authorities again carefully scrutinised her papers and cargo at a cost of a 24 hour delay to the vessel. Resulting from this incident and two others where British ships were intercepted the British Government made a formal protest to the Spanish insurgent naval authorities (the Nationalists) at Cadiz.

The situation in Northern Spain saw an offensive by the Nationalists starting early in April, 1937. The only means of getting supplies into the

North for the Basques was by sea, as all other means were closed due to Franco's success in isolating the region. As a result on April 6, General Franco announced that he would stop all ships from entering ports in Northern Spain, and set about stopping food getting to the Basques. There was already a shortage of food in the Northern territory and news of this blockade came as a considerable blow to them.

The Blockade of Bilbao caused a storm in Britain, where public opinion was firmly on the side of the Republicans and Basques. The political ramifications of the blockade are dealt with at length in my book *Welsh Blockade Runners in the Spanish Civil War* (1985). Briefly the Royal Navy advised the British Government that the blockade by the Nationalist Navy was effective, and as a result the Government instructed British shipowners, through the Board of Trade not to attempt to send ships to Bilbao. In fact any ship enroute to Bilbao was ordered to make for the French port of St. Jean de Luz to await further instructions.

As a result all those British merchant ships within 100 miles of Bilbao started to carry out the instruction given by the Board of Trade. The first ship arrived at St. Jean de Luz on April 8 and by the following day there were four vessels at anchor awaiting orders and developments. It was here that the legend of 'Potato' Jones was made. Of the four ships at anchor at St. Jean de Luz, three were Welsh owned, the *Marie Llewellyn* commanded by Captain David John Jones of Swansea and managed by Claude Angel of Cardiff, was loaded with potatoes destined for Santander, although there was a suggestion that her cargo concealed arms. Her cargo had come from Antwerp. Captain Owen Jones of Cardiff commanded the Guardian Line's *Macgregor* which had a general cargo consisting mostly of foodstuffs and grain. The Llanelli registered *Sarastone* with a cargo of foodstuffs, mainly potatoes and grain from Antwerp, was also commanded by a Captain Jones. The fourth vessel was the Newcastle owned *Hamsterley* loaded with foodstuffs and commanded by a Captain Still. The fact that three of the masters were named Jones prompted the international press to nickname them, and thereafter they became 'Potato' Jones *(Marie Llewellyn)*, 'Corn Cob' Jones *(Macgregor)* and 'Ham and Egg' Jones *(Sarastone)*.

Interest in the situation at St. Jean de Luz was widespread and was fuelled by the pretended sailings of one or more of the ships, and the rather outrageous statements of the masters, particularly 'Potato' Jones, who as a result will be remembered in history for his part, deserved or not.

The fifth ship to arrive was the Cardiff steamer *Seven Seas Spray* which was commanded by Captain William H. Roberts who lived at Okehampton, Devon. This ship was en route from Alicante with a general cargo which consisted of drums of olive oil, tinned foods, salt, barrels of wine, cognac, hams, horse fodder and other foods. When off the Spanish coast she was hailed by HMS *Blanche* and directed not to try to make for Bilbao, her intended destination, but to make for St. Jean de Luz instead. As she made her way along the coast she was met by the nationalist cruiser *Almirante Cervera* which escorted her past Bilbao, to ensure that she did not make for that port. This ship arrived at the French port on April 11.

Meanwhile Billmeir's steamer *Stanbrook* was making her way to this area commanded by a Captain Prance, and loaded with grain from the continent.

The *Sarastone* was later directed to Bordeaux for her cargo to be examined by the French authorities to ensure that she was not carrying any war materials.

At 4pm on April 15 the *Marie Llewellyn* suddenly and without warning weighed anchor and without permission or informing the harbour master set sail from the port. Speculation was aroused by her departure, as to her destination. 'Potato Jones' actually set out with the intention of running the blockade. However it was not to be, because as darkness fell he was intercepted by a British destroyer and turned back, returning to St. Jean de Luz the following morning. A day later he gave up his attempt to run the blockade altogether, and sailed for Alicante with his by now ruined cargo of potatoes.

On the night of Monday, April 19 at about 10pm the Cardiff registered steamer *Seven Seas Spray* weighed anchor at St. Jean de Luz and got under way with the intention of running the blockade. As she got near to the Spanish coast a British warship warned the master, but Captain Roberts declined to turn back, and carried on for Bilbao where he confounded everyone by arriving unmolested with his valuable and precious cargo intact.

His arrival at Bilbao was heralded by the local population, and the Basque Government even held a banquet in his honour, such was their gratitude.

The blockade having been broken, the British Government had to change their view. The Royal Navy thereafter informed British merchantmen that they would be protected outside territorial waters, and on the evening of April 22 the three ships still remaining at St. Jean de Luz set sail in convoy. These were the *Macgregor, Hamsterley* and Billmeir's *Stanbrook*. Unlike the *Seven Seas Spray* these ships had absolutely no chance of taking Franco's forces by surprise, who were well aware that the little convoy had set sail. On the morning of April 23 the Nationalist cruiser *Almirante Cervera* accompanied by the armed trawler *Galerna* were patrolling off the coast waiting for them. Fortunately and to no-one's surprise HMS *Hood* and HMS *Firedrake* were also in attendance. The Nationalist warships actually concentrated their attention on the *Macgregor* and warning shots were fired at her. However, the Royal Navy intervened and all three vessels managed to enter Bilbao intact with their precious cargoes.

Amazingly Captain Prance of the *Stanbrook* radioed Billmeir with, 'Arrived at 9.30am. Commenced to discharge immediately. Passage from St. Jean uneventful. No sign of mines or Franco. Everything in order and normal'. That was something of an understatement. Billmeir was well pleased that his ship had made it into Bilbao, as many of the cargoes destined for the port were undertaken through his brokerage.

Thereafter the Nationalists tended to leave the coast off Bilbao alone, and concentrated on the ports further to the West, including Gijon and Santander. The Royal Navy were instructed to patrol the area, and whilst powerless to intervene in Spanish territorial waters, did protect British merchant ships whilst outside the three mile limit.

At midnight on April 19 the Non-Intervention Committee's Naval patrol came into effect. This assigned the Mediterranean part of the Republic coast to Italy and Germany, the Basque/Santander coast to Britain, and the Nationalist held coast to both France and Britain. Non-Intervention Control officers were thereafter carried on ships going to and from Spain, thus ensuring as far as possible that arms were not carried.

The struggle by the Basques ended at Bilbao when the city fell to the Nationalists on June 19. Thereafter Franco concentrated his attentions on the ports to the West. Indeed Santander and Santona were to fall on August 25.

Numerous air attacks were now concentrated on Gijon and on August 26 the four British ships in the port were damaged by bombs. The vessels concerned were the Moller Line's *Hilda Moller*, the Cardiff managed *African Trader* and Jack Billmeir's cargo ship *Stanwood* and tanker *Stanbridge*. The masters of these ships now considered the ports of Northern Spain too dangerous and as a result the *Hilda Moller*, *African Trader* and *Stanwood* sailed from the port without delay. The *Stanwood* herself was only slightly damaged but most of her crew were shell-shocked. The ship arrived at La Pallice on the morning of August 29.

However the tanker *Stanbridge* was not so lucky. She had received damage which made her unable to weigh anchor, and she remained at Gijon trying to complete the discharge of her cargo under constant air attack for a further two weeks. Her valuable cargo of petroleum appeared to be the main target of the Nationalist aircraft. Damage to the vessel consisted of deck plates pierced, a direct hit on the port side No. 5 tank, transverse bulkhead between Nos. 5 and 6 tanks pierced and buckled, longitudinal bulkhead buckled. Tanks numbered 5, 6, 7 and 8 leaking heavily one to another either side. Shell plating pierced above waterline in several places. Discharge pipe on deck and steam pipes broken, lifeboats and bulwarks damaged slightly.

Repairs were effected to enable her to continue discharging her cargo, but on a later air attack she received a further two direct hits, which holed the forward and amidships decks, damaged the No 4 bulkhead and pumproom, broke the steering gear pipes and wrecked the midship section of the vessel. Fortunately only one member of the crew was injured, that being a greaser who was hit in the shoulder but only slightly hurt.

The master of the *Stanbridge* managed to effect repairs sufficiently to enable his valuable cargo to be discharged completely, and to enable the vessel to proceed to sea. The Nationalist grip on the port was tightening, and when the vessel left at 2am on September 10, she carried over 1,000 refugees on her decks, mostly being women and children. The vessel limped across the Bay of Biscay and arrived safely at La Pallice where she docked two days later. Temporary repairs were carried out and she was granted a certificate of seaworthiness in order to sail to Falmouth for a more thorough examination. Further repairs were effected there and eventually the ship sailed for the Tyne where she received permanent repairs at Smiths Dock.

At 10pm on September 8 the Billmeir steamer *Stanwold* was captured by an insurgent (Nationalist) warship within territorial waters off Rivadesella, Northern Spain, within sight of HMS *Resolution*. The *Stanwold* had been observed outside the three mile limit by the British warship, which had warned her that she was approaching territorial waters. Almost immediately after she crossed the three mile limit an insurgent torpedo boat which had been hovering on the horizon, gathered speed, overtook the *Stanwold* and fired three warning shots, The *Stanwold* altered course and proceeded accompanied by the torpedo boat, in the direction of Ferrol. When asked by HMS *Resolution* if he had anything to report, the master of the *Stanwold* wirelessed, "I am captured".

The Royal Navy were not happy with this case, as it was their belief that the master of the Billmeir ship had allowed himself to be captured deliberately. If that were the case Jack Billmeir would have dealt with him most severely. However after the cargo of the vessel had been confiscated, and repeated protests from the British Government the *Stanwold* was released by the Nationalists, and left Ferrol on November 1, 1937 and made for Bordeaux where the master communicated with Billmeir as to his future orders.

On September 13 the *Stanmore* (2) had left La Pallice in ballast chartered to the Republican Government to pick up refugees from Rivadesella. However the ship did not succeed in breaking through to the Spanish port, as when about five miles off the port she was attacked by insurgent aircraft which dropped bombs near the vessel, and the shore batteries opened fire on her. The *Stanmore* was not hit but the master wisely decided in the circumstances to return to France, arriving back at La Pallice on September 16.

Meanwhile in the South the *Sheaf Spear* which Billmeir had just bought, and which he was quick to resell, was lying at Tarragona when the port was attacked by three Italian Savoia-Marchetti aircraft, which dropped bombs all round the vessel, and although none scored a direct hit, shrapnel littered her decks. No one was injured but a number of crew members had to be treated for shock.

On October 20, the day before Gijon fell to Franco's forces, Billmeir's little steamer *Stangrove* of 516 gross tons with nearly 600 refugees on board was captured just after leaving the port by an armed trawler. However it became clear that the ship had made it to international waters and on the arrival of HMS *Southampton* on the scene in answer to the *Stangrove's* distress call, she demanded that the merchantman be released. The commander of the cruiser *Almirante Cervera* released the vessel under protest, and thereafter the *Southampton* escorted her from the war zone. Amazingly the ship had survived an air attack at the port the previous day when a direct hit had damaged her cargo of flour.

The *Stangrove* was actually the last vessel to leave Northern Spain before the war in the North came to an end on October 21, 1937 when Gijon, Musel and Aviles were taken by the Nationalists.

The war in the North might have ended, but not yet for the Billmeir fleet, as six days after the end of hostilities the little *Stanray* was captured by an insurgent armed trawler 3½ miles off Aviles. What she was doing there no one knows, but being outside territorial waters, the Royal Navy responded to her distress call and released her.

With the fall of Northern Spain British merchantmen concentrated on supplying the Republican Government through the Mediterranean coast ports. Jack Billmeir continued to employ his by now vast fleet of ships for the purpose where he earned considerable income.

6. FURTHER EXPANSION

At the height of the Spanish Civil War during 1938 Jack Billmeir added a further nine ships to the fleet of the Stanhope Steamship Co. Ltd., whilst a small number were disposed of or lost.

The *Stanburn* (1) formerly named *Hebburn* of 2,881 gross tons was acquired from Souter's of Newcastle. This ship was fourteen years old when bought. The 1,095 gross ton steamer *Dunstanburgh* entered the fleet as the *Stanburgh* from the Tyne-Tees Steam Shipping Co. Ltd. of Newcastle. This vessel had originally been built in 1912 for German owners as the *Greif*.

What was to be the most modern and pride of the fleet was the six year old *Kepwickhall* (4,831 gross tons) acquired from the West Hartlepool Steam Navigation Co. Ltd. This ship, a product of W. Gray and Co. Ltd., West Hartlepool, was renamed *Stanhall* (1). As can be seen it was often Billmeir's practice to incorporate a part of the former name of a ship in the name that he chose for it. The *Stanland* (1) of 1912 was acquired from Currie's of Leith. She was of 1,753 gross tons and had previously traded as the *Borderland*. The larger *Stockwell* (5,757 gross tons) came from Brocklebank's of Liverpool. She was built in 1914 and was renamed appropriately as *Stanwell* (1).

The 1923 built steamer *Stanlake* (1,742 gross tons) came from Watts, Watts and Company but had had a succession of previous owners. The 5,525 gross tons steamer *Arracan* of 1912 was bought from P. Henderson and Co. Ltd., Glasgow, and was renamed *Stanmore* (4). The coaster *Stancourt* (2) (965 gross tons) of 1909 was another acquisition from Currie's of Leith.

The largest ship to enter the fleet up to that time was the *Stanfleet* which had been laid down in 1920 by Barclay, Curle and Co. Ltd., Glasgow, as the *War Jupiter* for the Shipping Controller. A big ship of 7,951 gross tons with a large refrigerated capacity she had been completed as the *Otaki* for the New Zealand Shipping Co. Ltd., London, and had passed to the Clan Line in 1934 as their *Clan Robertson*.

A small passenger vessel, the *Queen of the Bay* was purchased during this year by the management company itself, J. A. Billmeir and Co. Ltd., but was quickly resold before trading, to French owners. She had a gross tonnage of 783.

As mentioned earlier the managed *Stancor* was repurchased during the year from her Latvian owners, and the *Stancroft* returned from the Greek flag after a short period.

Disposals accounted for the *Stancroft,* mentioned above, which was lost through hostilities in the Spanish Civil War, and the small *Stanray* which was sold for breaking up in Belgium. The *Stanthorpe* (1) was sold to Chinese owners, survived the Second World War and was broken up in Japan in 1953. The *Stancliffe* (1) was sold to Greek owners, also survived the war and was lost on March 16, 1951 two miles East of Sagres during thick fog whilst on a voyage from Aguilas to Pasajes with a cargo of esparto grass.

Another casualty of the Spanish conflict was the *Stanburgh,* which I will deal with later.

As can be seen Billmeir was operating a substantial fleet of ships, which included tankers, dry cargo vessels of the coaster, intermediate and large types plus a refrigerated ship of almost 8,000 gross tons. It was only four years since he had formed the Stanhope Steamship Co. Ltd., but at the end of 1938 the fleet still numbered twenty-one ships.

7. THE SPANISH CIVIL WAR—1938

Support for the Republican cause had come mainly from the Russians, and ever since the war had started they had been sending supplies, both war materials and foodstuffs consigned mostly in their own ships. The Russians had suffered heavy casualties at the hands of the Nationalist forces, with many of their vessels being sunk, damaged, captured and confiscated. From the start of 1938 the Russians declared to the Republican Government that whilst being prepared to provide the supplies she needed, they were no longer willing to risk their own merchant ships. Therefore if the Republicans wanted the supplies they would have to send their own ships to fetch them.

The main route for supplies reaching Spain from Russia was from Odessa in the Black Sea to the Mediterranean held ports. As a result of this ultimatum by Russia, the Republican Government set about chartering vessels to undertake what was clearly a hazardous voyage. Jack Billmeir was heavily involved with the supply of the Republican side, and when asked to help, felt obliged to risk his ships on the run.

Consequently it was no surprise when it was reported that the Billmeir steamer *Stanbrook* had left Malta on January 24, 1938 en route for Odessa in ballast. Franco knew what was going on and so did the Royal Navy. The Nationalists intensified their campaign against Merchant ships in the Mediterranean and the Royal Navy in an attempt to be seen to be doing their duty in an impartial way started checking cargoes of British ships to ensure if possible that no war materials and arms were carried in ships flying the British flag.

At this time a number of incidents occurred in the Mediterranean involving British flag ships. A number of merchant vessels had actually been torpedoed and sunk by submarines, suspected then and later proved to be Italian. The Italians had consistently supported Franco's forces throughout the conflict, and the attacks at sea by submarines only ended after a stern warning by the Royal Navy that any unidentified submarine found in the Mediterranean would be sunk without warning.

It was quite unusual for a Spanish merchant vessel remaining loyal to the Republic to make for a Spanish port. The usual practice was for the vessel to make for a North African port where her cargo would be transferred to a British owned vessel for the short dash across to Spain. On March 1, 1938 Lloyds reported that Billmeir's steamer *Stanbrook*, fresh from her voyage from Odessa to Spain, was taking the cargo of the Spanish steamer *Escolano* which had put into Bona harbour. Thereafter the British ship delivered the precious goods to the Spanish.

During February, 1938 the tanker *Stanmount* was lying at Valencia when the crew learned of Billmeir's intention of sending the vessel to the Black Sea to load at Odessa. They promptly went on strike, demanding a further 50 per cent increase in the danger rates of pay for the Spanish war zone. Eventually Captain John Roberts, her master, was able to make for Malta where they arrived on February 27. At this port the crew, having refused to continue the voyage to the Black Sea were paid off at their own request. They were repatriated to the United Kingdom at their own expense and the ship then signed on a Maltese crew for the remainder of the voyage.

On February 27 the *Stanwell* arrived at Tarragona with a cargo of 8,000 tons of coal from Newport, Monmouthshire, and was moored alongside the quay forming the southern arm of the inner harbour. At 4.30am on March 15 an air attack was carried out by an insurgent seaplane, flying at a height of about 300 feet. The *Stanwell* was obviously the target, as two bombs were dropped on the deck of the vessel, the first bomb dropped on the port side of the saloon, carrying away the bulwarks, iron decks, both main and 'tweendeck. The saloon and bridge then burst into flames. Steam was raised immediately and hoses connected, but water service pipes were useless owing to the damage. The fire spread to the bunker coal. The fire brigade arrived and by 7am the fire was under control. The master, chief officer, chief steward and the non-intervention officer were sleeping in the saloon at the time. Captain Davies of Cardiff, the master, gave orders for all hands to abandon ship owing to the fire. The second bomb was dropped on the port side after end of the firemen's forecastle, carrying away bulwarks and decks, both main and 'tweendeck, in No. 1 hold, and fracturing the vessel's side with a V-shaped crack from the main deck to a depth of 22 feet. The firemen's forecastle was completely gutted on the port side and the ship's side was pushed outward, steampipes were torn away and No. 1 hatch coamings flattened out.

During this period the wounded were carried ashore to the hospital. As a result of the attack, two men Messrs, Mulholland and King, firemen, both from Newport were killed, as was the Danish Non-Intervention Control Officer. Four other members of the crew were seriously injured. The chief officer and chief steward were also slightly injured. Temporary repairs had to be effected before the ship could be towed from the port to be repaired. The crew were housed ashore after the attack as the accommodation was destroyed. They refused to reboard the vessel and demanded repatriation home.

This was one of many attacks being carried out by aircraft. Clearly they were designed to hamper supplies to Republican ports, by dissuading owners from sending their ships into ports where considerable danger existed, and to interrupt the actual cargo working on the ships themselves. The insurgents felt that the disabling of a ship was a bonus which obviously supported the main objective.

On April 25 four British ships were damaged at Valencia during an insurgent air attack. These were the Blue Star Line's *Celtic Star* with one killed and three wounded, Billmeir's ship *Stanland* with the death of one of her crew, the Claude Angel vessel *Fredavore* and Stone and Rolfe's *Isadora*. All were fairly badly damaged, but Billmeir's ship had suffered most. All the ships survived and eventually were able to proceed from the port.

Barcelona was the target of insurgent aircraft on April 30. The port receiving two attacks, Nearly all the twelve British merchant vessels in the port were damaged by shell splinters. One member of the crew of the *Stanbrook* was wounded and was taken to the English Hospital at Barcelona for treatment. The force of the explosions was so terrific that two of the ships were lifted up and dashed against the quay.

On May 5 the *Stanhall* was hit by shrapnel during an air raid on Valencia. Her hull above the waterline, deck, superstructure and also under the counter was damaged. However she was able to leave port without effecting repairs. The *Stanwold* also received some damage during this attack, and was further damaged in an attack which occurred two days later.

It was becoming clear to all concerned that the merchant ships were being singled out as targets by insurgent aircraft. As a result the masters were registering protests with the British authorities. The steamer *Stanhope* (2) in this later attack was at anchor outside the harbour when two bombs fell withing 10 yards of her, but fortunately damage was minimal.

Republican territory was cut in two when Franco's troops reached the Mediterranean in April 1938. The first major port in the region to fall to the Nationalists in this determined thrust, was Castellon on June 15. This level of activity by the Nationalist forces saw an increase in attacks on merchant vessels. This division of Republican territory presented a major problem to them and to those, who by now were virtually all British, who were prepared to carry their supplies. Indeed transport between the two regions held by the Republic was also carried on British ships. By now most of the supplies reaching the government were being transhipped at Oran or Marseilles from vessels not prepared to run the gauntlet, into other ships, of which Jack Billmeir's were predominant. These ships ran a feeder service into Spain, and obviously taking greater risks were handsomely rewarded. The instances of damage were far more numerous than had previously been the case.

The Royal Navy were very concerned to be seen to be doing their duty properly. For some time past they had suspected that British ships were on occasions carrying war materials to the Republic in direct contravention of the Merchant Shipping (Carriage of Munitions to Spain) Act, 1936. As a result on occasions British ships were taken into port and examined in detail. On other occasions they acted on complaints made by Franco or the Non-Intervention Committee who had Control Officers on board every vessel entering or leaving Spain. Jack Billmeir, who was in fact the major shipowner involved in the trade was bound to provoke some attention. His ships were watched very closely throughout the conflict, and he became a legend to those involved, particularly the crews of his ships.

Early in May the *Stancroft* had left Barcelona with a general cargo destined coastwise for Valencia. On arrival at Valencia the Control Officer on board had complained to the Royal Navy that the vessel was carrying munitions, and as a result the vessel was ordered out of the port by the Navy, as it was considered inappropriate to investigate the complaint on the spot. As soon as the ship, commanded by Captain Stanley Scott, left the port a Naval Guard was put on board from HMS *Hyperion,* and the vessel brought to Gibraltar for examination. She was moored at the Gun Wharf of HM Dockyard, where her cargo was discharged and examined. It was found that she was carrying cartridge cases, aeroplane engines and other articles of war.

Billmeir was horrified when he heard that his vessel had been detained, and on hearing that his master had been charged before the Police Court at Gibraltar with the offence of 'taking and carrying munitions of war to Spain', and granted bail of £100 with two sureties in the same sum, he immediatey despatched Mr. D. N. Pritt, KC., MP., to defend him.

Meanwhile the cargo of the *Stancroft* of which 95 per cent was not of articles of war, was restowed in the vessel, with the exception of the munitions. A new master, Captain S. L. Spence arrived in Gibraltar to take over command, and later the ship was allowed to leave making straight for Valencia.

The Republican Government then made a formal complaint to the British Government that the cargo on board the vessel, including the war equipment was their property and by ordering the vessel out of Valencia, had indeed been seized on Spanish territory. A claim was made for the seized cargo to be returned. The complaint, however, fell on deaf ears.

The trial against Captain Scott proceeded, and evidence was given for the prosecution by the Non-Intervention Control observer and the ship's Second Officer to the effect that the master was privy to the munitions being on board. However the defence made the submission that there was no case to answer on the following grounds:—
(1) No evidence of goods going to Valencia.
(2) Goods conveyed between Spanish ports not subject to Non-Intervention Agreement.
(3) Master not privy to contraband on board.
(4) Charge discloses no offence.

Counsel for the Crown replied that goods and munitions carried to Spanish ports came under the Act, also that the master was privy to carriage of prohibited goods.

However, the Court decided that there was no case to answer on the grounds that the prohibited articles were being conveyed from one Spanish port to another, and Captain Scott was discharged, with no order made as to costs, Billmeir was jubilant.

The *Stanray* was proceeding towards Valencia, when at 2 am on June 9, off Gandia, she was machine-gunned by a seaplane. The seaplane circled the vessel twice and poured a stream of bullets at her, but fortunately her aim was bad and no harm was done by the attack. The ship arrived at Valencia on the morning of June 10 without further incident.

The fall of Castellon on June 15, 1938 gave the insurgents a base in between the Republican held territory, and eventually they pushed further to the North. The increase in air attacks was alarming to many of the British merchant ship masters, and as a result, even before the fall of Castellon seven of them had lodged a protest with the British Consul on June 10 concerning the air attacks on their vessels at Barcelona. This protest was forwarded to the Foreign Office in London. It was made by Captain C. Lewis of the Billmeir steamer *Stanburn* and Captain G. Davies of the *Stanbrook* which had been involved in a number of incidents under Billmeir's houseflag during the conflict, together with the masters of the steamers *Gothic, Hamsterley, Sea Glory, Alex* and *Kenfig Pool.* However the attacks continued unabated.

On June 22 the *Stanwold* arrived at Gibraltar, where the master reported having had a blank shot fired at his ship by a Nationalist trawler whilst he was sailing down the Spanish coast, but he had declined to stop for the insurgent vessel.

It was interesting to note the list of repairs which the *Stanhall* required following her bombing in May. It was far more serious than had been expected, and only became fully apparent when she was dry docked at Baltimore. It consisted of renewing twelve plates, one off and six fair, frames, beams, brackets, bulkheads, stringers, and deck plating straighten and renew, seams caulk, tanks test, hold ceiling part renew, deck fittings repair, rudder recondition, propeller blades straighten, draw shaft, and repairs to electrical lighting, together with sundry lighting. This was the pride of Jack Billmeir's fleet and he was none too pleased.

On June 27 the British steamers *Laleham, Bramden* and *Stanwold* (Billmeir's) were hit by flying shrapnel during an air raid at Alicante. During this attack the steamer *Farnham* was sunk by a direct hit.

Two of Billmeir's steamers were damaged on July 19 while lying at Valencia. The *Stanland* was set on fire by a bombing attack by five insurgent aircraft. The damage was actually caused by a bomb landing in 250 drums of gasoline which were on the quay having been unloaded from the vessel. The bridge was set on fire and part of the accommodation scorched quite badly. However, the fire was put out after about an hour and on completion of discharging the vessel she was able to proceed to Oran for temporary repairs. At the same time the *Stangate* which was across the harbour from the *Stanland* was slightly damaged by shrapnel, when a bomb fell between the ship and an air raid shelter. Her master, Captain Bibbings from Cardiff and the majority of the crew were fortunately ashore at the time. The ship arrived at Marseilles on July 26 for survey, but repairs were not necessary.

The *Stanleigh* was the next of Billmeir's ships to be damaged. On July 28 she was hit by a bomb whilst lying at Valencia. The raid was undertaken by six Savoia aircraft and fifteen buildings were hit as well as the port church. Two members of the *Stanleigh's* crew were injured, neither seriously. The bomb fell on the poop, penetrated to the storeroom and started a fire, which the crew put out before any serious damage could be caused.

At 2am on July 28 the *Stanwold* arrived at Gibraltar en route from Cathagena to London with a cargo of oranges. She had to put into port to effect temporary repairs following her sustaining damage at Alicante. The repairs to her steering gear and bridge took several days and the ship finally left Gibraltar on August 1 at 6pm for London.

The *Stanleigh* was attacked a second time whilst lying at Valencia, when on August 5 during an air raid two bombs landed between the vessel's hull and an air raid shelter. Numerous holes were blasted in the bridge, the chart-room was wrecked and a splinter a yard long was hurled into the engine-room where, however, the damage was not serious.

Such was the level of air attacks on Republican held ports that air raid shelters had been erected in port areas. When an air raid commenced the stevedores, dock workers and ships' crews would quickly leave the ships and take refuge. Indeed some ships' crews were actually being housed ashore, where possible, away from the most dangerous areas, when cargo was not being discharged. This constant volume of air attacks created long delays and congestion in port, and instead of ships being able to discharge their cargoes in days or up to a week, the time in port was extended in cases up to two or three weeks. This made the job of carrying cargo to and from the Republic even more dangerous. A good number of the ships engaged in the trade were now operating what amounted to a feeder service from Marseilles and Oran, whilst ships nor prepared to take such risks were discharging at those ports instead of running the gauntlet.

The British Government made repeated protests to General Franco about these air attacks, although it was clear that in addition to insurgent aircraft, German and Italian forces were also involved. In one reply General Franco published a list of vessels which, he claimed were British and had been carrying munitions for the Barcelona (Republican) Government. It was claimed that since January 1, 1937 more than 200 ships flying the British flag had attempted to carry contraband to Republican ports. The same reply also mentioned the names of a number of companies which it claimed were engaged in the arms traffic to Spain. Franco stated:

Britain has an easy remedy to stop the bombing of her merchant vessels, this is by prohibiting the use of the British flag to protect the undignified contraband traffic in arms in the Republican zone. Nobody doubts the final outcome of the war. Why try to lengthen Republican resistance?

The majority of British ships were lawfully engaged in carrying cargoes of foodstuffs and other materials, and lifting fruit for export from the Republic and since the date quoted indeed about 200 British ships had been trading to the Republic, but they were not all, if any, engaged in carrying arms. The British Government had given strict instructions that the Royal Navy were to keep a close eye on this aspect, and whilst no doubt a few took a chance, it was very isolated. Only one case was ever taken to trial, that being the master of a Billmeir ship, and he had been acquitted.

The Nationalist Government went on to list British ships which it alleged were engaged in carrying munitions to the Republic. Of the twelve ships listed, one had to be from Jack Billmeir's fleet, as follows:

Stanburgh — Left Amberes for Valencia May 15 with cargo suspected to include 20 million cartridges. (Ship owned by the Stanhope Steamship Co. Ltd., London, Manager J. A. Billmeir).

The statement also gave a list of British companies which it said were shipping materials to Republican Spain.

Stanhope Company, which owned only two ships before the Spanish war; and today owns nineteen.

Billmeir Company, which organised the Stanhope Company, and formed five other companies for the same trade. These (it claimed) were the Westcliff Shipping Company, Thameside Shipping Company, Veronica Steamship Company, Dillwyn Steamship Company, and Trent Maritime Company, all of which were formed after the Spanish war started. The name of the Mid-Atlantic Company was also given.

In relation to the shipping companies Franco had almost got it right, other than the fact that Billmeir did not have a financial interest in the later five. He did, however, act in most cases as cargo brokers for all of them. Clearly the allegations about specific ships were rather wild, and as one would predict provoked a howl of protest from the owners of the

36

companies concerned. However, it is interesting to note that Jack Billmeir said nothing.

Most of the cargo being carried to Republican Spain was consigned in British ships. The Republicans were still receiving arms and clearly someone was carrying them. Readers will have to form their own opinion.

At 11.30am on August 11 the *Stanlake* was damaged during an air raid at Valencia, when she was raked with machine-gun bullets, and a number of bombs landed near her. There were no casualties among the crew, but the ship was holed in several places above the waterline, and her two lifeboats were damaged.

Eight days later, on August 19 the *Stanforth* which had just left Barcelona for Oran was attacked by an aircraft when 15 miles off the coast. Fortunately the bombs missed, there was no damage, and the vessel continued on her voyage.

The legendary little *Stanbrook* was not to be so lucky that day. She was the subject of an air attack whilst lying at Vallcarca, to the South of Barcelona. In the first of two raids, a bomb landed on the bridge and another in No. 1 hold causing a hole in her hull. The ship started to sink slowly, but the crew's attempt to beach her failed. The ship was further damaged in a second raid, causing another hole below the waterline, adjacent to No. 2 hold. The ship settled by the head, listing heavily, until she had rested on the bottom. However, although her cargo of cement was ruined, the ship was refloated on August 23 and towed to Barcelona, where she was dry docked and successfully repaired. There had been no casualties amongst the ship's personnel.

In another air raid at Barcelona on September 16 four British steamers were damaged, including Billmeir's *Stanlake* which had her poop smashed and her hull holed, fortunately above the waterline.

On September 24 the *Stanholme* was quite badly damaged by bombing at Barcelona. Her midships section and stern were badly smashed, and her mainmast had gone over the side due to the amount of damage caused by the attack.

On October 13 the *Stancroft* was severely damaged when a bomb scored a direct hit on the vessel at Barcelona. The bomb landed on her after deck and part of the deck was destroyed and a fire started which took half an hour to extinguish. The vessel sprang a leak, and her master, Captain Leonard Spence, of Redcar, Yorkshire, instructed his crew to take their belongings ashore before the vessel settled on the bottom. During the same attack the *Stanholme* was further damaged, having all her doors and part of the bridge blown away. She was not however, in a sinking condition.

Valencia suffered a heavy insurgent air attack on the evening of November 1, when three waves of bombers flew over the city at 7pm, 9pm and 11.20pm. During the attack the steamer *Stangate* was struck by bomb fragments but the extent of the damage was not severe.

Two days later the *Stanburn* was hit whilst lying at the same port. A bomb fell in her No. 1 hold and made a hole in her hull below the waterline. The vessel in leaking condition was pumped out and temporary repairs effected. The Chief Engineer was slightly injured, and her precious cargo of foodstuffs was removed before it could be spoiled. The vessel was, after repairs able to proceed.

The *Stanburgh* was not so fortunate, as on November 4 whilst lying at the French port of Etang de Thau, Sete, she was ripped apart by an explosion whilst loading petrol destined for Spain. So severe was the damage that the vessel had to be abandoned, and subsequently sold for breaking up where she lay.

The *Stanwold* was at this time operating a feeder service from Oran to Valencia. On November 14 she was slightly damaged during an air attack at Valencia, but arrived back at Oran three days later. Eight days later the *Stanwold* back in Valencia again was badly damaged in an attack which also damaged three other British merchantmen. Again after effecting temporary repairs she was able to leave, and on November 28 headed for Marseilles for a more thorough examination.

On November 28 two Billmeir ships were damaged by air attack at Barcelona. These were the *Stanwell* and *Stangrove*. A bomb hit the deck of the *Stanwell* squarely, penetrating below, where it exploded, badly perforating the vessel's side. The explosion wrecked the forecastle quarters, starting a small fire which was quickly extinguished. The deck equipment, winches and forward mast were damaged and the steam connections severed, but temporary repairs were subsequently made. Two other bombs narrowly missed the vessel, one falling in the water astern and the other on the quay. The *Stanwell* was unloading a cargo of coal. The *Stangrove* was slightly damaged by fragments when a bomb hit the quay alongside her.

The steamer *Stanhall* had for some time, being Jack Billmeir's, pride and joy, been kept out of the Spanish war zone since the damage caused to her during an air raid some time earlier. It was now something of a surprise to see that Billmeir was involved in carrying cargo for another conflict. He was not a man to miss opportunities. On November 26 it was reported that the *Stanhall* was unloading a cargo of 6,000 tons of arms and ammunition for China. At this time a conflict was ensuing between the Chinese and Japanese, and indeed the Japanese were fighting and taking Chinese territory. The cargo of arms had been carried on the *Stanhall* from Russia, and part of the cargo was sent by rail to Lashio, a Burmese town, 18 miles from the Chinese frontier, and thence by road to China, while the rest, consisting of explosives, was shipped up the Irrawaddy by boat to Bhamo, 40 miles from the border and thence by road.

The Chinese were having trouble getting supplies through to their troops and clearly Jack Billmeir was their man. In this instance there was absolutely no pretence as to the nature of the cargo. There was no law in the United Kingdom to prohibit the carriage of arms for the Chinese, and Billmeir did his best to satisfy their requirements. A number of his ships were to be involved in the trade, but these tended to be his more modern and larger vessels, where the risks of interception by the Japanese Navy, although very real, was less risky than those in the Spanish conflict.

Returning to the Spanish Civil War, the number of attacks on Republican held ports by insurgent aircraft had increased considerably. In line with this activity, the instances of damage to Jack Billmeir's ships had also increased. On December 1 the crew's quarters of the *Stanwell* were damaged by a bomb whilst the vessel was lying at Barcelona. Two days later the *Stanland* also at Barcelona was holed below the waterline and had her crew quarters destroyed by a bomb during an air raid. Fortunately none of the crew were injured, as they were now spending more time ashore, either being housed ashore or taking refuge in air raid shelters.

On December 5 at Barcelona the *Stanwell* was badly damaged on the starboard side by a bomb. She was one of three ships hit during an air raid, the others being the *Transit* and *Noemijulia*. In a further raid later that day the *Stanwell* was again hit, as was her consort *Stanhope* and the *Transit* and *African Mariner*. The valiant *Stanwell* whilst still at Barcelona was to survive further attacks on December 6 and 10, which increased the amount of damage suffered by the vessel. It was a wonder that some of these Billmeir owned ships could still float.

On December 14 the *Stanholme* was entering the port of Valencia with a cargo of coal when she was hit by shrapnel during an air attack.

Having been severely damaged on October 13 at Barcelona the *Stancroft* had been successfully raised and was in the process of being repaired when a further blow befell the vessel. As on December 27 she was again bombed at Barcelona, and once again the ship sank at her moorings. Unfortunately Barcelona was under seige by now and was under almost constant air attack. As a result there was no way that Billmeir could get her raised and repaired and she had to be abandoned. On April 19, 1939, some three months after the Nationalists took Barcelona she was successfully raised and subsequently repaired by them. Thereafter she was renamed *Castillo Almansa*, placed under the Spanish flag and traded as such for many years.

. Knowing how Franco and his forces felt about Jack Billmeir and his valiant fleet of ships it was no surprise that Billmeir never saw his ship again. It is quite clear that Billmeir was a thorn in the side to the Nationalists, and without his intervention and support the Republicans would not have survived thus far. Franco knew this.

8. THE SPANISH CIVIL WAR—1939

In relation to the Civil War British shipowners were actually earning enhanced freight rates to engage in the trade. Many historians have asserted that owners such as Jack Billmeir were earning double their normal profits. I contend that this is not so, they were actually earning something like double their gross freight. Simply defined this meant that a profit of say £200 on a freight of £2,500 prior to the civil war or on a voyage not connected with the trade, returned on a voyage to or from Spain during the conflict something like £2,700 on a gross freight of £5,000. Clearly the returns were very good. It was no wonder that Billmeir was still prepared to run the blockade even with the high instances of damage through insurgent bombing. Whilst Billmeir was prepared to risk his ships it is clear that his crews were also prepared to take the risks associated with the trade, in view of the enhanced pay that they were receiving.

At the start of 1939 it was clear to everyone, and none more so than Billmeir, that the Republican resistance would not last too much longer, and whilst he was still running his fleet of ships in supplying them he did not increase his fleet as in the previous two years. However during the early part of the year he did acquire one additional vessel. This was the 5,817 gross ton refrigerated cargo steamer *Clan Grant* from the Clan Line. She had been built in 1912 for the Port Line as the *Port Macquarie,* later passing to William Thomas Shipping as their *Cambrian Marchioness,* before entering the Clan Line fleet in 1928. In the Stanhope Steamship Co. fleet she became *Stangrant.*

Returning to the conflict in Spain, on January 14, 1939 the legendary *Stanwell* was again damaged by an air attack while lying at Barcelona. She received serious damage to her superstructure and accommodation, and both sides of the vessel's hull were riddled above the waterline. A fire started but the flames were quickly put out by the crew and the local fire-service. On the same day the *Stanforth* received damage to her bridge house and her hull during an air raid at Carthagena. But she proceeded to Gibraltar for survey of the damage and temporary repairs.

On January 22 the port of Valencia was again under insurgent air attack, five Savoia bombers being involved which dropped about fifty bombs. On this occasion the Billmeir steamer *Stanholme* was hit by shrapnel which badly damaged the plating on the port side of her stern.

A day earlier the last Billmeir ship to leave Barcelona before the city fell to the Nationalists, the *Stanbrook* departed. She had only managed to cover seven miles when she was subjected to three air attacks in the space of an hour. In the first she was attacked by seven aircraft and as a result the vessel turned back. However after a short space of time she resumed her voyage to be attacked by five aircraft and again by a further three. The Nationalist air force couldn't have been that good because they did not score a single hit and the vessel, undamaged was subsequently escorted into Port Vendres by an Admiralty tug.

Barcelona fell to Franco's forces on January 26 but fortunately the much damaged *Stanwell* had managed to depart a few days earlier and made for Marseilles where repairs were immediately put in hand. The territory still remaining in Republican hands actually bordered Madrid in the West, Valencia in the North and Almeria to the South, and included Carthagena and Alicante. But still Billmeir continued to supply the Republicans.

On February 5 the little *Stangrove* was making her way along the Spanish coast outside territorial waters with a cargo of mercury, sulphur, nitrate potash and nitrate ammonia en route from Valencia to Port Selva, when she was bombed and machine-gunned by insurgent aircraft. As a result her master, Captain Richards of Whitchurch, Cardiff, gave instructions to the crew to abandon ship and take to the lifeboat, remaining himself on board. The aircraft then disappeared and the master ordered the lifeboat's return. Owing to the rough sea then running the lifeboat was wrecked. The following day an insurgent destroyer hove in sight and, after firing warning shots at the *Stangrove*, ordered her to stop. A guard of eleven armed men was then sent on board the vessel and she was taken into Barcelona, which was now in insurgent hands, where a number of the crew were taken into custody. Later the vessel was ordered to proceed to Palma, Majorca, to which port she sailed under an armed escort. Whilst lying at this port the ship was wrecked during a gale on February 23. However the Spanish salved her in 1941 and placed her into their fleet as the *Castillo del Oro,* and she survived thereafter until 1971 when she was delivered to shipbreakers in Spain.

During an air raid on Valencia on February 9 the *Stanbrook* and *Stanforth*, which were in the process of unloading foodstuffs, were damaged by shrapnel. Ten days later while lying at Almeria the *Stanburn* was hit by shrapnel during another air attack by the insurgents.

On March 8, 1939 the Nationalist Forces announced a blockade of all the Mediterranean Spanish ports, as follows:—

> The whole of the Mediterranean coast of Spain between Adra and Sagunto is closed for navigation to all kinds of ships of whatever nationality and whatever kind of cargo; no ships should approach it without the proper authorisation of the Admiral in Chief of the blockade force of the Mediterranean within a distance of three miles. Any ship not observing these instructions will be seized. Navigators are warned that off the fortified base of Carthagena and along the stretch of coast between the Torre de Mesa Light and Cabo Palos there will be submarines with orders to sink any ship which attempts

to approach the coast within the three mile limit, no matter what the nationality of the ship may be. Ships proceeding with cargo for other ports on the coast in the 'Red' zone, whatever their nationality, should go to ports in liberated Spain, preferably Barcelona, Palma, Majorca or Malaga.

This in effect declared another blockade, but by now the war was all but over. However, there were still a few British ships in the zone at this time, including some owned by the by now legendary Jack Billmeir.

At 9.32pm on March 10, the Welsh steamer *Bellwyn* gave out the following distress call.

Bellwyn, position Cape San Antonio bearing 170 degrees; 23 miles distant; ordered to Palma, Majorca, by warship. Immediate assistance. Steamer *Stangate* under escort, proceeding to Palma, Majorca. (Remainder of transmission jammed.)

At 10.24pm the following message was sent by the *Bellwyn,* addressed to all British warships.

Refused to submit, now left alone. Please rescue steamer *Stangate* being taken to Palma, Majorca.

Apparantly the *Stangate* was en route from Valencia to Almeria to load a cargo of oranges destined for London, and was in company with the *Bellwyn* when they were both ordered to stop by a Nationalist warship. Both ships tried to make for the coast and evade capture, but the *Bellwyn* was more fortunate, as the warship, predictably, concentrated her attentions more on the Billmeir ship. The *Bellwyn* had refused to submit, but the *Stangate* was captured by the insurgent ship. As a result of the *Bellwyn's* distress message the Royal Navy sent the destroyers HMS *Intrepid* and HMS *Impulsive* to investigate. They found the *Stangate* making for Majorca under escort of the insurgent warship, and immediately demanded her release, which they achieved without any incident or problems. The ship was then escorted to Gibraltar.

Due to the intensity of the Nationalist blockade, when the *Stancor* left Valencia on the night of March 14 with 200 refugees on board she was escorted by the cruiser HMS *Devonshire* to ensure that the British merchantman was not interfered with.

On March 16 the Billmeir steamer *Stanhope* left Gandia for Gibraltar, and having made it out into International waters (outside the three mile limit) she was intercepted by a Nationalist warship who directed her towards Palma, and commenced to escort her. The merchant ship's radio operator only managed to get off a short distress call, "British steamer *Stanhope* in distress" before her radio was jammed. However the Royal Navy sent HMS *Sussex* to investigate, and when found she secured the release of the Billmeir ship. Thereafter, when the Spanish vessel was out of sight the *Stanhope* was instructed to proceed on her way, unescorted. There were no further incidents on the ship's passage to Gibraltar.

Having been released by the Royal Navy on March 10, the *Stangate* ever cheeky, was again stopped off the Spanish coast by an insurgent warship which placed an armed guard on board, and then escorted her to Palma. On this occasion she was not so lucky, as the Royal Navy were unable to locate her to intervene. However after the fall of the Republic the vessel was released and allowed to proceed from the region.

On March 29 Valencia surrendered to General Franco's forces, and on the following day the last ship to leave Spain, the Billmeir steamer *Stanbrook* departed from Alicante with 1,800 refugees on board. The last stronghold of Republican resistance Almeria, Carthagena and Alicante fell to the Nationalist forces on March 31, and the civil war officially ended on April 1, 1939.

It was fitting that the last British merchantman to give service to the Republic had been Jack Billmeir's legendary steamer *Stanbrook* which had also been one of the first to reach Bilbao two years earlier.

The conflict had lasted for a total of thirty-three months and the participation of British merchant ships had clearly helped to stiffen the Republican resistance. Without the supplies carried by these ships, and in particular Billmeir's huge fleet, the civil war would have ended far earlier; Franco was well aware of this, and had frequently complained about it. As a result of the intervention, General Franco banned any merchant vessel which had traded with the Republic, from entering Spanish ports thereafter. Jack Billmeir knew this would happen, but was in a very good position to secure the future of his fleet, having amassed a considerable fortune, which as I will show he used to good effect.

Following the end of the Spanish conflict, Billmeir set about repairing and modernising his fleet of ships. During the period of months before the Second World War broke out he disposed of five vessels.

The tanker *Stanbridge* was sold to German owners and during the Second World War was used by the Germans as a supply ship under the name *Eurofeld* until on September 24, 1944 she was scuttled at St. Nazaire. The ancient tanker *Stanfield* (1) was immediately sold for breaking up, having served her purpose. The *Stanmore* (4) was sold to Latvian owners, but was wrecked at Bordeaux in 1947. The large refrigerated *Stanfleet* passed to the Blue Star Line as their *Pacific Star* and was lost through enemy action in 1942, whilst the *Stancourt* (2) of 965 gross tons was sold to Panamanian interests, and was also to fall victim to enemy action in the war.

Jack Billmeir had never owned a new ship, and following the Spanish Civil War he had certainly amassed sufficient capital to enable him to invest in new tonnage. As a result when on March 28, 1939 the British

Government announced plans to support British shipowners by introducing the British Shipping (Assistance) Bill, 1939 he decided to take advantage of the scheme. This Bill provided loans to shipowners ordering new tonnage in British yards, and further, offered a grant to the shipyard securing the order. With the resources that Billmeir had, it was really unneccessary for him to use the scheme, as it was felt more appropriate for owners who had been experiencing the lean years following the depression of the 1930s. Billmeir had, since forming the Stanhope Steamship Co. Ltd. in 1934 in fact been trading at well above the average profit margin.

However he did take advantage of the scheme, and in the Spring of 1939 ordered a 4,970 gross ton steamer from W. Pickersgill and Sons Ltd., Sunderland. The ship which was capable of a service speed of 10.5 knots was to be fitted with engines by G. Clark (1938) Ltd., also of Sunderland. The purchase price of the vessel was £122,346, of which Billmeir was granted a loan by the govenment of £97,500 at very favourable terms.

At the outbreak of the Second World War on September 3, 1939, the fleet comprised of the following vessels:—

Name	Year Built	Gross Tons	
Stanholme (1)	1927	2,473	
Stancor	1904	790	
Stanhope (2)	1919	2,337	
Stanleigh	1912	1,802	
Stanbrook	1909	1,383	
Stanwold	1909	1,019	
Stanwood	1915	4,158	
Stangate	1912	1,289	
Stanmount	1914	4,468	(tanker)
Stanforth	1915	1,817	
Stanburn (1)	1924	2,881	
Stanhall (1)	1932	4,831	
Stanland (1)	1912	1,735	
Stanwell (1)	1914	5,757	
Stanlake	1923	1,742	
Stangrant	1912	5,817	

9. THE SECOND WORLD WAR

At the outbreak of hostilities the sixteen ships owned by Jack Billmeir's Stanhope Steamship Co. Ltd. were all trading. The smaller units were engaged in the coastal and intermediate trades whilst the five larger vessels were engaged in deep sea voyages, mostly by this time to and from the River Plate, outwards with coal and home with grain.

In addition to the sixteen ships in the fleet at the outbreak of war, seventeen vessels were acquired, nine of which were built to Billmeir's own order. Of these a total of seventeen ships were lost directly as a result of enemy action, whilst two were lost through normal marine hazard, and a further two were sold to the Admiralty. In addition of the many ships managed on behalf of the Ministry of War Transport, eleven were also sunk.

The first ship to fall victim to the enemy was the legendary little *Stanbrook* which under the command of Captain Dickson left Antwerp on November 18, 1939, bound for the Tyne in ballast, struck a mine and sank with the sad loss of her entire crew of twenty-one.

The next loss was not through enemy action. The *Stanwood* was on a voyage from Methil to the River Plate via Dakar when on December 10, 1939 she put into Falmouth Roads for bunkers, and was at anchor when her cargo of coal caught fire. She was towed clear of other shipping, and an attempt was made to extinguish the fire by flooding her holds. Unfortunately as this was being done the vessel suddenly sank with the result that the radio operator who was asleep in his bunk at the time was lost. The ship became a total loss, although over the years much of the wreck has been salved for scrap.

Fifteen days later, on Christmas Day, the *Stanholme* (1) commanded by Captain Hook, was mined and sunk in the Bristol Channel with the tragic loss of thirteen members of her crew. Captain Hook and twelve other men being rescued.

During 1940 the *Stanland* (1) was sold to the Admiralty for use as an ammunition hulk, and remained afloat employed as such until 1951 when she was sold for breaking up at Milford Haven.

Five ships joined the fleet during this year. The newbuilding on the stocks at W. Pickersgill and Sons, Sunderland, as their yard number 243 was launched on May 22 and given the name *Stanmore,* incredibly being the fifth ship in Billmeir's fleet to carry the name in six years. She was completed in August and promptly handed over to the company. Also acquired were the *Stancliffe* (2) of 4,511 gross tons which was bought from Lambert Bros. Ltd., London. This ship was a modern tramp steamer, having only been completed in 1936 by Lithgows Ltd., Port Glasgow. The three year old *Stanpark* (1) (5,103 gross tons) joined the fleet from Chas. C. Dunn Shipping Co. Ltd., Liverpool, whilst the older *Parracombe* (4,698 gross tons of 1928) and *Welcombe* (5,122 gross tons/1930) came from Pyman Bros Ltd., West Hartlepool and entered Billmeir's employment without change of name.

As the war at sea intensified so did the losses suffered by the company. On January 29, 1940 the *Stanburn* (1) was bombed and sunk off Flamborough Head with the loss of twenty-five men, including her master, Captain Lewis. There were only three survivors. On April 12 the newly acquired *Stancliffe* (2) was torpedoed and sunk 45 miles North East of Uist Island, Shetlands, by the German submarine *U37* while on passage from Narvik to the United Kingdom with a valuable cargo of iron ore. Four days after the sinking a lifeboat from the ship containing survivors in an exhausted condition reached a Scottish port, but unfortunately twenty-two men including Captain Sudbury, her master, were lost.

The next loss suffered by the company was Billmeir's pride and joy, the steamer *Stanhall,* which on May 30 was torpedoed and sunk by the German submarine *U101* in position 48.59N, 05.17W, while homeward bound from Australia to the United Kingdon, via Suez, with a cargo of sugar. One member of her crew was lost. Six days later the coaster *Stancor* was shelled and sunk by the submarine *U48* which conducted the attack on the surface, in position 58.48N, 08.45W.

The *Stanwold* was more fortunate, as on September 15 whilst lying at Southampton Docks she was bombed and damaged during an attack by German aircraft. After repairs she was able to resume her service in the fleet. The last loss suffered during 1940 was the *Stangrant* which was torpedoed and sunk by the submarine *U37* North West of St. Kilda, whilst in convoy, with the loss of eight crew. Her master, Captain Rowlands was among the survivors. The submarine responsible was the same one that had claimed the *Stancliffe* (2) six months earlier.

Jack Billmeir had decided, even during the war, to use some of the capital which he had accumulated as a result of the Spanish Civil War, to build a considerable number of vessels to his own order. The *Stanmore* which was ordered prior to the outbreak of the conflict, was followed by orders for a further eight vessels. Of the nine ships built to his order during the war, eight came from the yard of W. Pickersgill and Sons Ltd., Sunderland, and one from Bartram and Sons Ltd., of the same port. As a result of this close connection with Sunderland, he became identified with the local community, and donated £1,000 to the local hospital.

The second newbuilding to Billmeir's order, the *Stanford,* having been ordered from Pickersgill's on October 4, 1939 was launched on October 3, 1940 as the builder's yard number 245. She was completed early in 1941, and was the only ship to enter the Stanhope fleet during that year.

The next loss was the *Stanpark* (1) which had been in the fleet for barely a year. On January 19, 1941 she was en route from Bombay with a cargo of cotton destined for the United Kingdom when she was intercepted by the German Pocket Battleship *Admiral Scheer* and captured. The crew were taken prisoner, and the *Stanpark* was sunk by gunfire from the warship. Eventually the Billmeir ship's crew were landed in occupied territory and were to spend the remainder of the war in Germany as prisoners of war.

On February 27 of that year, the *Stanwold* under the command of Captain MacCready, whilst in convoy from the Tyne to Cowes with 1,300 tons of coal, was seen to have a heavy list. As there was a heavy sea running, and conditions were very bad the Billmeir ship dropped out of sight of the convoy. Nothing more was heard of the ship or her crew of nineteen and two gunners until bodies of some of them were washed up in Pevensey Bay. The Admiralty finally agreed to apportion the loss as 60% war and 40% marine.

On March 14, the *Stanleigh* in ballast, and in convoy on passage from Devonport to Workington under the command of Captain Bibbings was bombed and sunk in the Irish Sea by German aircraft with the tragic loss of her master and sixteen members of crew, there only being six survivors. Less than a month later on April 4, the steamer *Welcombe* on passage from the United States to the United Kingdom with a full cargo of grain, was torpedoed and sunk by the German submarine *U98* with the sad loss of half of her crew.

In the early Summer of 1941, beleaguered Malta was calling for urgently needed food and war supplies and the enemy was making it impossible for merchant ships to get through even in escorted convoys. Remembering Jack Billmeir's record during the Spanish Civil War, the Admiralty approached him, and asked him to use his experience to try and get supply ships through to Malta. Billmeir agreed to make the attempt, and chose the steamer *Parracombe* to make the initial venture. The ship, heavily loaded with foodstuffs and all manner of war supplies, left Methil and sailed coastwise to Oban where she joined a Southbound convoy. When off Gibraltar the ship was detached from the convoy and escorted to a point near the Straits where she was left to make the attempt to get through to Malta, alone. With one of Billmeir's most experienced masters aboard and a Spanish master to act as Pilot, the ship was quickly disguised as a Spanish merchantman and took a course which skirted the North African coast. An Italian aircraft flew over the ship, and the master feeling that the pilot had been satisfied by the disguise, felt more confident. However on May 6 the ruse had been seen through by the Italian forces and the ship was bombed and sunk with the tragic loss of thirty of her brave crew. The survivors were picked up by a French (Vichy) seaplane and landed in French North Africa where they were to spend many months incarcerated in very poor conditions. Eventually they were released, together with the crews of other unsuccessful ships making the attempt later under Billmeir's directions, and were repatriated. On arrival in Britain, Jack Billmeir, realising that they had suffered a terrible ordeal, paid out of his own pocket for each man to be fitted out with a new suit of clothes. A small, but well received token of his appreciation for what the men had been through.

On September 6 of the same year the last remaining tanker in the Stanhope Steamship Co. Ltd. fleet, the *Stanmount* was attacked by German aircraft off Great Yarmouth, and received damage when a bomb landed on the vessel. However following repairs the vessel returned to service, but unfortunately three months later on Christmas Eve while on a voyage from London to Grimsby she sank off Yarmouth having struck a mine. At the time she was loaded with creosote.

Meanwhile Billmeir was still trying to get supplies through to Malta. For this purpose he had allocated five managed vessels. Unfortunately there was to be a heavy loss of life, but he did succeed in getting one ship to Malta on his final attempt. Thereafter the supplies were taken in heavily escorted convoys under Admiralty supervision using fast cargo liners. Of the ships which made the attempt under Billmeir's directions, the *Empire Guillemot* (5,641 gross tons, built 1919) was sunk by an aircraft torpedo West of Galeta Island on October 24, 1941; the *Empire Pelican* (6,463/1919) was sunk on November 14 by an aircraft torpedo between Galeta Island and Tunisia; whilst the *Empire Defender* (5,649/1910) which had been in company with the *Empire Pelican* was sunk in similar fashion on the following day. The final loss whilst undertaking this hazardous voyage was the *Empire Barracuda* (4,296/1918) which was torpedoed and sunk by the German submarine *U77* before she reached the Mediterranean.

However it was with a sense of great pride that Jack Billmeir learned that the managed steamer *Empire Gull* (6,408/1919) had reached Malta early in 1942 with her much needed cargo. The courage of the men manning all these ships was beyond question. It was tragic to think that so many had died in the attempt, but their efforts had not been completely in vain, as one ship did actually make it, and she too had made the attempt completely unescorted.

Unfortunately another Billmeir ship was lost before the end of 1941 by marine hazard. This was the steamer *Stangate* which on December 7 sank off the Wash following a collision with the Greek steamer *Agios Georgios* while on passage from the Tyne to Portsmouth with a cargo of coal.

Five ships were to join the fleet during 1942. These were the *Raby Castle* (4,996/1925) from the Lancashire Shipping Co. Ltd., Liverpool, which due to wartime regulation kept her original name, and four newbuildings

The steam coaster "Stanmore" dating from 1918 was one of two vessels acquired by the Stanhope Steamship Co. Ltd. in 1934 on its formation.

(E. N. Taylor).

Dating from 1904 the "Stancor" was bought in 1936. She is shown during 1937 whilst flying the Latvian flag for a short period. (John Clarkson).

The "Stanhope" (2) of 2,337 gross tons, was acquired in 1937.

(Laurence Dunn).

The "Stanleigh" of 1912 joined the fleet in 1937.

(Laurence Dunn).

The "Stanbrook" was bought in 1937, and was involved in a number of incidents with Nationalist Forces during the Spanish Civil War. (York Collection).

The "Stanray" which had been built in 1904 was acquired in 1937. She was broken up a year later.
(Welsh Industrial & Maritime Museum).

The "Stanthorpe" (1) joined the fleet in 1937 and was sold a year later.

(John Clarkson).

Bought in 1937, the "Stanwood" was lost by fire at Falmouth in 1939.
This view shows the wreck.

(Laurence Dunn).

Acquired in 1938 the "Stanland" (1) was sold to the Admiralty in 1940 for use as an ammunition hulk.   (Laurence Dunn).

The "Stanlake" joined the fleet of the Stanhope Steamship Co., Ltd. in 1938. She is shown under her earlier name of "Ruckinge". (Welsh Industrial & Maritime Museum).

The "Stanfleet" of 7,951 gross tons was acquired in 1938 and sold a year later.

(A. Duncan).

The "Stanmore" (5) of 1940 was the first ship built for the Stanhope Steamship Co. Ltd. She is shown under tow after having been torpedoed in the Mediterranean on October 1, 1943. She was subsequently beached and declared a total loss.

(Laurence Dunn).

Another view of the torpedoed "Stanmore", with "ML469" alongside.

(Laurence Dunn).

The "Stanford" was built in 1941 by W. Pickersgill and Sons Ltd., Sunderland.

(Skyfotos Ltd.)

The "Stanford" of 1941.

(Welsh Industrial & Maritime Museum).

The "Stanhall" (2) of 1925 was bought in 1942.

(A. Duncan).

The "Stanridge" was built in 1943 by W. Pickersgill & Sons Ltd., Sunderland.

(Welsh Industrial & Maritime Museum).

The motorship "Stankeld" of 1937 was acquired in 1944.

(Welsh Industrial & Maritime Museum).

The "Stankeld".

(A. Duncan).

The "Stanrealm" was built in 1944 by Bartram & Sons Ltd., Sunderland. (Welsh Industrial & Maritime Museum).

The "Stanrealm".

(Skyfotos Ltd.).

Acquired in 1944, the "Stanpark" (2) was only one year old.

(Welsh Industrial & Maritime Museum).

The "Stancourt" (3) of 1924 was bought in 1944.

(Welsh Industrial & Maritime Museum).

The tanker "Stanbell" was acquired in 1945 from the Ministry of War Transport.   (Welsh Industrial & Maritime Museum).

The "Stanbell" after conversion into an ore carrier in 1955.

(Tom Rayner).

The "Stancliffe" (3) wrecked at Sharpness in 1947.

The "Stancliffe" (3) was abandoned to salvors, and subsequently refloated and repaired at Cardiff.

The tanker "Stanglen" was acquired in 1946 and sold in 1952. In 1954 she was re-purchased and renamed "Stanpark" (3).
(A Duncan).

The Victory ship "Stanmore" (6) was bought and sold in 1947.

(Welsh Industrial & Maritime Museum).

The tanker "Stanmore" (7) was two years old when bought in 1947.

(Tom Rayner).

The "Stanmore" (7).

(A. Duncan).

The tanker "Stanwell" (2) joined the fleet in 1947.

(Skyfotos Ltd.).

The "Stanwell" (2) in ballast.

(Skyfotos Ltd.)

The tanker "Stanwell".

(Welsh Industrial & Maritime Museum).

The war-built "Stanway" of 2,902 gross tons was acquired in 1948.

The "Stanfirth" was bought in 1948 from the Admiralty and converted for commercial service.

(A. Duncan).

The "Stanfirth" was a unit of the fleet from 1948 until 1961.

(Tom Rayner).

The 9,136 gross ton "Stanroyal" was acquired in 1948. She had been built in Germany in 1929.

(A. Duncan).

The "Stanroyal".

(Tom Rayner).

The "Stanburn" (3) was built in 1951 by the Burntisland Shipbuilding Co. Ltd.

(A Duncan).

The "Stanburn" (3) was sold to Russia in 1954.

(Tom Rayner).

The "Westford" of 1941 joined the fleet of Duff, Herbert & Mitchell Ltd. in 1954. She is shown under her earlier name of "Paris City".
(Tom Rayner).

The Tanker "Westbrook" built in 1942 was bought in 1955.

(Skyfotos Ltd.)

The "Elstead" was acquired in 1955 and placed in the ownership of J. A. Billmeir & Co. Ltd.

(Skyfotos Ltd.).

The "Elstead" was built in 1943.

(A Duncan).

The "Stanland" of 1942 was bought from W. H. Seager & Co. Ltd., Cardiff in 1955. (Welsh Industrial & Maritime Museum).

The "Stanfield" was bought in 1955 and converted from a tanker into an ore carrier. (Skyfotos Ltd.).

The tanker "Stanloch" was bought in 1955.

(Skyfotos Ltd).

The "Stanthorpe" (3) was acquired in 1955.

(Skyfotos Ltd.)

The "Stancrown" was built in 1956 by J. Crown & Sons Ltd., Sunderland.

(Tom Rayner).

The "Stancrown" of 1956.

(A. Duncan).

The "Stanwear" was built in 1956 by W. Pickersgill & Sons Ltd., Sunderland.

(A. Duncan).

The "Stanwear" of 1956.

(Skyfotos Ltd.).

The "Westbay" was acquired by Duff, Herbert & Mitchell Ltd. in 1957 and sold in 1962.

(Skyfotos Ltd.).

The tanker "Stanvale" was built in Sweden in 1957 and sold later that same year.

(A. Duncan).

The tanker "Stancloud" (12,700 gross tons) was built at Newcastle by Swan Hunter & Wigham Richardson Ltd. in 1958. She was the largest and last ship to join the fleet.

(A. Duncan).

delivered from the yard of W. Pickersgill and Sons, Sunderland, as follows:—

Name	Gross tons	Launch date	Yard No.
Stangarth	5,966	21.10.1941	250
Stanbank	5,966	18.12.1941	251
Stancleeve	5,970	4. 5.1942	253
Stanhill (2)	5,969	30. 6.1942	254

On March 12, 1942, the *Stangarth* under the command of Captain Herbert, was one day out from New York on passage for Table Bay and India, and still on her maiden voyage, when she was torpedoed and sunk by the Italian submarine *Morosini* with the loss of her entire crew of forty and six gunners. The loss of this ship which had so recently entered the fleet was a blow to Billmeir, but the loss of her crew was a far greater tragedy. However a further blow was to occur, when on May 5 of the same year the *Stanbank* was torpedoed and sunk by the German submarine *U103* South East of New York. Again this ship was on her maiden voyage, and sadly nine of her crew of forty-nine were lost. Her master, Captain Niddrie was among the survivors, who after ten days were picked up by the Blue Funnel Line's *Rhexenor* and landed at Bermuda.

On May 14, only nine days after the loss of the *Stanbank*, the Belgian steamer *Brabant* (2,438/1938) which was managed by Billmeir on behalf of the Ministry of War Transport, was torpedoed and sunk by the German submarine *U155* in position 11.32N, 62.43W. Less than a month later on June 6, the managed Yugoslavian vessel *Susak* (3,889/1927) was torpedoed and sunk in the Indian Ocean by the Japanese submarine *I-16*. Another loss was the managed *Norton* which was sunk by air attack whilst lying at Bari Harbour.

The last casualty during 1942 was the *Empire Gull* which had made it through to Malta earlier in the year. On December 12, she was torpedoed and sunk in the Indian Ocean by the submarine *U177*.

During 1943 two new ships arrived from the yard of W. Pickersgill and Sons Ltd., as follows:—

Name	Gross tons	Launch date	Yard No
Stanlodge	5,977	9.11.1942	256
Stanridge	5,975	22. 3.1943	258

On January 1, 1943 the managed ship *Empire Panther* (5,600/1919) was lost when she was mined off Milford Haven when inward bound from the United States. On April 14, of the same year the *Stanlake* was attacked by E-boats and torpedoed and sunk twelve miles South of Lizard Head. The crew having taken to the boats were picked up by an escort vessel and landed at Falmouth. Within 48 hours of landing, her master, Captain Purvis, was at sea again in command of the *Stanforth*.

On July 9 the *Stanhope* (2) was attacked by German aircraft while in position 37.10N, 09.00W, and although damaged by a bomb was successful in making port where repairs were carried out. The steamer *Empire Lake* (2,852/1941) was not so lucky, as on July 15 whilst on passage from Durban to Aden she was torpedoed and sunk by the submarine *U181*. Unable to launch the ship's boats, the crew took to the rafts. Five survivors arrived at Madagascar on August 2.

Whilst on her Maiden voyage the *Stanridge* under the command of Captain Niddrie was attacked off Gibraltar by an Italian Assault craft and severely damaged. Captain Niddrie refused to abandon ship, and the ship managed to make port where she was patched up, thus enabling her to cross the Atlantic to the United States where more permanent repairs were carried out.

On October 1, 1943 whilst taking part in the invasion and supply of Sicily, the modern, and indeed the first ship ever built for Billmeir's Stanhope Steamship Co. Ltd., the *Stanmore* (5) was torpedoed by the German submarine *U223* in position 36.41N, 1.10E, while on passage from Middlesbrough with a cargo of military stores. The decision was taken to tow her in, and she was beached at Tenes. However, the damage was so great that she was declared a Constructive Total Loss.

Four ships were acquired by Jack Billmeir during 1944. The newbuilding *Stanrealm* of 7,062 gross tons was built as Yard No. 300 by Bartram and Sons Ltd., Sunderland, to the company's own order. She was launched on April 25 of that year, and was soon in service with the company. She was built by Bartram's because the Pickersgill yard, were unable to build her due to their full order book.

The acquisitions were the *Dunkeld* (4,956/1937) from Dunlop's of Glasgow, the one year old motor vessel *Jersey Hart* of 7,275 gross tons from Morel Ltd., Cardiff, which were the first motor ships to enter the fleet, and the *Framlington Court* (5,026/1924) from the Court Line Ltd., London. The quality of the tonnage entering the Stanhope Steamship Company's fleet was first class, many of the second-hand purchases being very modern. This was in stark contrast to the ships which made up the fleet during the Spanish conflict. It was clear that Jack Billmeir had his eyes to the future. Even though his fleet had suffered at the hands of the enemy, he had always set about replacing losses.

Whilst Billmeir had always operated the fleet from offices in London at 9, St. Helen's Place, E.C.3., during the war he moved the major part of his management team to temporary accommodation in Cheltenham, Gloucestershire. Whilst there he met and befriended Richard Street, the principal behind the well known South American Saint Line of Cardiff, who at that time had temporary accommodation in the Wye Valley.

During 1944 the *Stanwell* (1) was sold to the Admiralty for use as a blockship at the Normandy Beach Head. Also allocated for such use was the *Empire Tamar* (6,640/1907) which had previously been managed by Billmeir on behalf of the Ministry of War Transport.

The final loss suffered by the company was the managed steamer *Empire Lough*, (2,824/1940) which on June 24, 1944 whilst taking her third cargo of explosives to the beach-head was intercepted and attacked off Dover. Her master, Captain Robinson remained aboard until all his crew were safely in the boats and then jumped into the sea himself. However, sadly he died a short time later.

For their part in the war, the following decorations were awarded to personnel of the Stanhope Steamship Co. Ltd.

DSO	Two
OBE	Ten
MBE	Four
DSC	Fifteen
DSM	Seventeen
BEM	Six
Mentioned in Despatches	Nine
Commendations	Twelve

10. THE IMMEDIATE POST-WAR PERIOD

At the conclusion of hostilities the fleet of the Stanhope Steamship Co. Ltd. comprised of the following vessels:—

Name	Year Built	Gross Tons
Stanhope (2)	1919	2,337
Stanforth	1915	1,817
Stanford	1941	5,969
Stancleeve	1942	5,970
Stanhill (2)	1942	5,969
Stanhall (2) ex *Raby Castle*	1925	4,996
Stanlodge	1943	5,977
Stanridge	1943	5,975
Stankeld ex *Dunkeld*	1937	4,956
Stanrealm	1944	7,062
Stanpark (2) ex *Jersey Hart*	1943	7,275
Stancourt (3) ex *Framlington Court*	1924	5,026

This represented a fine modern fleet. But it is the composition of the fleet which is of the greatest interest. In 1939 out of sixteen ships only five were deep-sea tramps of 4,500 gross tons and over, whilst the other eleven were either coasters or intermediate tramps. In 1945 out of twelve ships in the fleet, ten were out and out tramps, and only two were of the intermediate trade type, whilst there was no longer any coasters in the fleet. This was obviously achieved by Billmeir by design. It is apparent that he intended to run larger and certainly more modern ships than before the war. However, he was a clever man, who tended to regard his ships as assets which were always for sale if offered the right price. The subsequent pages will clearly show this.

There had not been a tanker in the Billmeir fleet since the *Stanmount* had been lost during the war, so it was no surprise when in 1945 the first acquisition following the war was the 'Norwegian' type tanker *Empire Beresford* from the Ministry of War Transport under the British Government's Ship Disposal Scheme. This ship with a gross tonnage of 9,804 had been completed two years earlier by Sir James Laing and Sons Ltd., Sunderland, and entered the fleet as the *Stanbell*. She was used by Billmeir mostly on the spot market which following hostilities was pretty buoyant, as there was very little tonnage which was free from government control at that time.

Unfortunately during that same year the *Stanforth* was wrecked on August 17, at Grundkallegrund while on passage Kalix to London with a much needed cargo of timber. This was a sad loss to Billmeir, as even though there had been no casualties among the crew, this was one of the two ships which had survived throughout the war, and was in fact one of the ships which had served him so well during the Spanish Civil War.

Four ships were acquired during 1946. The tanker *Empire Chancellor* (9,917 gross tons/built in 1945) was purchased from the Ministry of War Transport, and was renamed *Stanglen*. In addition the *Empire Ortolan* (4,970/1919) an American Hog Island ship, and the *Empire Brook* (2,852/1941) a 'Scandinavian' type intermediate tramp came from the government also, as the *Stanland* (2) and *Stancliffe* (3) respectively. An interesting ship which entered the fleet was the American built *Coity Castle* (2,767/1919) which had previously been owned since 1939 by the Branch Steamship Co. Ltd., which was managed by Reginald Jones of Cardiff, another stalwart of the Spanish conflict. This ship had been beached at Dagenham since November 27, 1944 following a collision in the River Thames. Billmeir always with an eye for a bargain bought her as she lay, from the Salvage Association to whom she had been abandoned. He paid to have her refloated and repaired and took her into the fleet as his *Stanburn* (2). In addition he acquired the small ex-Naval vessel *Lexamine* which he converted as a Cadet training ship. Billmeir obviously intended to have the best personnel possible, and was prepared to train up his own men, starting with Cadets.

Unfortunately within months of acquiring the *Stanburn* she was lost, as on October 27, 1946 she sank after striking a submerged object North of Kerkehah Bank in position 35.15N, 11.55E, while on passage from Algiers to Sfax in ballast. Fortunately there were no casualties amongst the crew.

During 1947 Billmeir took delivery of five ships which had been constructed in the United States as part of the war effort. Two of these were fast 'Victory' ships of approximately 7,600 gross tons built in 1945 for the United States Maritime Commission by Bethlehem Fairfield Shipyard Inc., at Baltimore. These were by no means tramp steamers, they were fast vessels, and were more in the category of a cargo liner. Billmeir was lucky to have been able to have bought them, and it was no surprise therefore when within a few months they were both sold to the mighty P. and O. Company for use on their liner trades. The ships had carried the names *Stanholme* (2) and *Stanmore* (6) in the fleet, and were sold at considerable profit.

Also acquired was the 7,242 gross tons 'Liberty' ship *Samskern* which had been built in 1944 at the same yard as the two 'Victory' ships. She was a more suitable vessel for a tramp shipowner, and was renamed by Billmeir as the *Stanthorpe* (2).

The other two ships were both 'T2' tankers of 10,700 gross tons which had been built in 1945 by the Sun Shipbuilding and Dry Dock Company, at Chester, Philadelphia. These ships brought the number of tankers in the fleet to four, and were actually the biggest ships to have entered the Stanhope fleet up to that time. They were given the names *Stanmore,* the seventh to carry that name, and *Stanwell* (2).

This year was to be an unlucky one for Jack Billmeir, as he lost two ships through marine hazard. After no more than a year trading for him, the *Stancliffe* (3) on April 3 was abandoned after grounding North West of North Pier, Sharpness Dock, in the River Severn, while on passage Emden to Sharpness with a cargo of timber. The ship broke in two and was declared a Constructive Total Loss, although her timber cargo was saved. Subsequently the wreck was sold, and both parts of the hull were refloated, towed to Cardiff and rejoined. Thereafter in 1948 the ship was trading as the *Gripfast* for the Newbigin Steamship Co. Ltd., of Newcastle, a company which had also been involved in the Spanish Civil War trade. She later changed hands a number of times, and on December 6, 1967 sank in position 13.32N, 55E, after developing leaks while being towed from Djibouti to Colombo by the salvage tug *Nisos Kerkyra*. The other loss was the war built *Stanhill* (2) which a month later, on May 11 was wrecked off the Ivory Coast, while on passage from Lagos to Glasgow with a general cargo.

Three ships were acquired during 1948. Billmeir had been managing the 2,902 gross tons 'Scandinavian' type tramp steamer *Empire Record* for two years, and when the opportunity presented itself he bought the ship, which was renamed *Stanway*. He bought the Admiralty Aircraft Engine Repair ship *Beauly Firth* of 7,285 gross tons which had been built in 1944 by J. Readhead and Sons Ltd., South Shields. After conversion to commercial service at considerable cost the ship was placed in the traditional tramp trades as the *Stanfirth*. Also acquired was the German built *Isar* of 9,136 gross tons. This ship built in 1929 for the Norddeutscher Lloyd of Bremen was an unusual ship with four imposing masts, and had been taken over by the British Government following the war. Again Billmeir spent a considerable sum on refitting her and then placed her in service as the *Stanroyal.*

No ships were disposed of during 1948, but the following year the *Stanland* (2) and the *Stanthorpe* (2) were sold for further trading. The *Stanland* became the *Alma* under the Panamanian flag, and traded for a further four years, as on March 31, 1953 she arrived at Milford Haven for breaking up. Billmeir was offered a good profit on the *Stanthorpe* which he had only owned for two years, from the Larrinaga Steamship Co. Ltd., of Liverpool, who were trading a number of these 'Liberty' ships. Thereafter she became the *Domingo de Larrinaga,* and was resold in 1955. Eventually on January 6, 1969 she went aground off Constanza in heavy weather and was abandoned, while on a voyage from Alexandria to Constanza.

The only transaction during 1950 was the *Stanhope* (2) which had been the only ship left in the fleet which had been involved in the Spanish conflict. She was sold to German owners and traded until on December 11, 1957 she arrived at Hamburg for breaking up.

As far back as 1947 Billmeir had placed orders for two new motor ships, one with Short Bros. Ltd., Sunderland, and the other with the Burntisland Shipbuilding Co. Ltd. of Burntisland, Fife. They were both completed during 1951 as the *Stanhope* (3) of 6,034 gross tons and the *Stanburn* (3) of 5,575 gross tons. They had been the first newbuildings to join the fleet since the war, and Jack Billmeir was well pleased with them. With their arrival the fleet comprised of the following vessels, although as I will show, a number were sold in the next twelve months at considerable profit.

Name	Year Built	Gross Tons
Stanford	1941	5,969
Stancleeve	1942	5,970
Stanhall (2)	1925	4,996
Stanlodge	1943	5,977
Stanridge	1943	5,975
Stankeld	1937	4,956
Stanrealm	1944	7,062
Stanpark (2)	1943	7,275
Stancourt (3)	1924	5,026
Stanbell	1943	9,804 (tanker)
Stanglen	1945	9,917 (tanker)
Stanmore (7)	1945	10,708 (tanker)
Stanwell (2)	1945	10,722 (tanker)
Stanway	1942	2,902
Stanfirth	1944	7,285
Stanroyal	1929	9,136
Stanhope (3)	1951	6,034
Stanburn (3)	1951	5,575

In addition the Cadet Training Ship *Lexamine* (129 gross tons/built 1946) was still in commission.

11. PROFIT TAKING

At the outset of 1951 the fleet managed by Jack Albert Billmeir, through his Stanhope Steamship Co. Ltd comprised eighteen vessels, most of which were comparatively modern. The composition of the fleet was four tankers and fourteen tramps, of which only one was not for world wide trading, i.e. the 2,902 gross tons intermediate tramp *Stanway*. This represented a considerable achievement by Billmeir, and one of which he was understandably and justifiably proud. However he was a shrewd man, and the most profitable years following the Second World War were those during the 1950 to 1953 Korean War. During this conflict a situation existed where there were not enough ships to carry the world's trade. The additional demands for tonnage made by this war resulted in the freight market shooting up. Billmeir was able to take advantage of this, and earned some excellent returns with his fine fleet of ships. But being a clever man he knew that no upsurge in the freight market ever lasted for long, and so he decided to take full advantage whilst at its height by disposing of a high proportion of his ships whilst the price being paid was so artificially high. Ships were changing hands at two and three times that which they had cost even a few years earlier, and in some cases for even more than that. He decided to sell and keep some reserves for the future with which to invest in ships when the price of them was back to something like normal. He also decided to take some of the profits out of the business, as I will show later.

During the height of the boom, he sold eleven of his eighteen ships, five during 1951 and six the following year, and made, as was by now his way of doing business, a fortune. The *Stancleeve* was sold in 1951 to Norwegian owners for whom she traded as the *Akera* for a further ten years before being broken up. The *Stanhall* (2) went to Japanese owners via Hong Kong interests and was broken up in 1962 in Japan, whilst the *Stankeld* had a succession of owners before being scrapped in 1970. The *Stanpark* went to other British owners initially, and she too was to have a long career being broken up in 1970. The *Stanway* had no less than five further owners before being broken up in 1966.

Of the six ships disposed of during 1952 the three sisterships *Stanford*, *Stanlodge* and *Stanridge* all went to the Indian flag, and had been broken up by 1965. The *Stancourt* (3) was sold to Hong Kong interests, and after a number of changes of ownership was scrapped in 1958, whilst the German built *Stanroyal* went to Turkish owners and was subsequently broken up during 1965. The tanker *Stanglen* passed to London Greek owners as the *Newminster* but returned to the Billmeir fleet two years later.

Having disposed of over half the fleet this left the following vessels:—

Name	Year Built	Gross Tons
Stanrealm	1944	7,062
Stanbell	1943	9,804 (tanker)
Stanmore (7)	1945	10,708 (tanker)
Stanwell (2)	1945	10,722 (tanker)
Stanfirth	1944	7,285
Stanhope (3)	1951	6,034
Stanburn (3)	1951	5,575

Having accumulated a considerable fortune, Jack Billmeir decided to put the Stanhope Steamship Co. Ltd. into voluntary liquidation in order to take some of the profits. As a result on February 7, 1952 the company was wound up, and the remaining ships together with certain other assets were transferred to a new company, originally registered on January 26, 1952 as the S.S. (St Helen's) Ltd., but which was changed on the date of the liquidation of the Stanhope Steamship Co. Ltd. to that same name. Shareholders in the new company received one fully paid up share of £1 for every 5s 0d share and also received £2 1s 8.94d cash for every share held in the old company. This represented a considerable sum of money, and as Jack Billmeir and his wife were the principal shareholders, most of this actually went to them.

The following year the management company — J. A. Billmeir and Co. Ltd. was also wound up, and a new company of the same title formed. This transaction actually came into effect on March 31, 1953. At this time both companies were trading from offices at 9, St. Helen's Place, London, EC3.

An interesting transaction took place during 1954 when a new company was acquired. This was Duff, Herbert and Mitchell Ltd., of 116, Fisherton Street, Salisbury, Wiltshire. This company had been formed in 1945 and had originally been managed by C. A. Lenson from offices at 5, Bevis Marks House, 23-24, Bevis Marks, London EC3., but in 1949 management had passed to Owen T. Williams of Port Dinorwic, North Wales. The original fleet of this company had comprised of five coasters, *Dawlish* (248 gross tons/built 1937), *Alfred Mason* (305/1919), *Juliet Duff* (502/1920), *Veronica Tennant* (484/1922) and the *Joseph Mitchell* (650/1918). It is interesting to note that the *Juliet Duff* which they had acquired in 1946 had originally been Jack Billmeir's pioneer vessel *Stanhope* when he had formed the original Stanhope Steamship Co. Ltd. in 1934.

However, when Billmeir acquired the company he did not take any of the vessels, which by that time had all been sold. The new company operated from an office at 3, Stanley Street, Liverpool, 1, although management was again entrusted to J. A. Billmeir and Co. Ltd.

The first ship owned by Billmeir to be registered under this company, was the *Paris City* of 7,084 gross tons which was bought from the Leeds Shipping Co. Ltd. (Sir William Reardon Smith and Sons Ltd.), of Cardiff, although she had originally been built in 1941 by Vickers-Armstrong Ltd., Barrow as the *Empire Baxter* for the Ministry of War Transport. Under Billmeir's management she became the *Westford*.

During 1954, having spent two years trading as the *Newminster* for London Greeks, the tanker formerly in the fleet as the *Stanglen* was re-acquired, and renamed *Stanpark* (3). At about the same time, having served her purpose the Cadet training ship *Lexamine* was disposed of.

During 1954 W. Gray and Co. Ltd., of West Hartlepool were fitting out a newbuilding for the Stanhope Steamship Co. Ltd. This ship, which had been launched as the *Stanpool,* was a steamer with a proposed gross tonnage of 7,347. Jack Billmeir who always had an eye for a profit, was approached by the Russians who were anxious to acquire some modern tonnage. As a result he sold the new ship to them together with the pair of ships built to his order in 1951. The *Stanpool* was completed for the Russians as the *Bogdan Khmelnitsky* and is still trading as such, whilst the *Stanhope* (3) and *Stanburn* (3) entered Russian service as the *Sovetskaya Artika* and *Zapoljarje* respectively. The former vessel has not been heard of this side of the iron curtain for some years, so it is not known whether she is still afloat, however the former *Stanburn* was broken up in Pakistan in 1979.

The freight market having dropped back, and the price of ships having fallen considerably, Jack Billmeir considered that the time was right to start building his fleet up during 1955. Apart from orders which had already been placed for the construction of two large tankers and two tramps, six ships were bought from other owners during this year. Since the Korean War when the cost of importing iron ore into the United Kingdom had been so high, even if ships could be chartered to carry it, the British Iron and Steel Corporation (B.I.S.C.O.), had set about chartering purpose built or converted vessels for this purpose to ensure that they could receive adequate and continuous supplies. As a result Billmeir purchased the 10,420 gross tons tanker *Thamesfield* from Hunting and Sons Ltd., Newcastle, and converted this ship which he renamed *Stanfield* and his own tanker *Stanbell* into ore carriers for charter to B.I.S.C.O.

Also acquired were the tankers *Alan Evelyn* (8,137/1942) and *Vivien Louise* (9,912/1944) from Stevenson, Hardy and Company's British Oil Shipping Co. Ltd., which entered Billmeir service as the *Westbrook,* named after his home in Surrey, for Duff, Herbert and Mitchell Ltd., and the *Stanloch* for the Stanhope Steamship Co. Ltd. Two cargo ships entered the Stanhope fleet as the *Stanland* (3) (7,162/1942) from Seager's of

Cardiff, and the *Stanthorpe* (3) (7,033/1944) from London Greek owners, whilst the *Elstead* (7,061/1943) was formerly owned by J. and C. Harrison's of London. This last ship which was given the name of the village where his house Westbrook stood in Surrey, was placed in the ownership of the management company—J. A. Billmeir and Co. Ltd.

During 1956 the two cargo tramps on order for the company were delivered, they were the 8,002 gross ton motor ship *Stancrown* from J. Crown and Sons Ltd., Sunderland, and the *Stanwear,* a motor ship of 8,108 gross tons from W. Pickersgill and Sons Ltd., also of Sunderland. They were an excellent pair of ships which were above average for use in the tramp trades.

During the Suez Crisis of 1956 the ships traded at considerable profit, as the shortage of tonnage brought about by the short term closure of the canal became apparent. However, on this occasion Billmeir was satisfied to continue trading the fleet and did not sell any ships. It is interesting to show the fleet, which had more than doubled in four years.

STANHOPE STEAMSHIP CO. LTD.

Name	Year Built	Gross Tons	Type
Stanrealm	1944	7,062	Cargo Tramp
Stanbell	1943	10,341	Ore Carrier
Stanpark (3)	1945	9,917	Tanker
Stanmore (7)	1945	10,708	Tanker
Stanwell (2)	1945	10,722	Tanker
Stanfirth	1944	7,285	Cargo Tramp
Stanfield (2)	1943	10,420	Ore Carrier
Stanland (3)	1942	7,162	Cargo Tramp
Stanloch	1944	9,912	Tanker
Stanthorpe (3)	1944	7,033	Cargo Tramp
Stancrown	1956	8,002	Cargo Tramp
Stanwear	1956	8,108	Cargo Tramp

DUFF, HERBERT AND MITCHELL LTD.

Name	Year Built	Gross Tons	Type
Westford	1941	7,084	Cargo Tramp
Westbrook	1942	8,137	Tanker

J. A. BILLMEIR AND CO. LTD.

Name	Year Built	Gross Tons	Type
Elstead	1943	7,061	Cargo Tramp

In 1957 the *Westford* was sold for further trading to Liberian interests, and was eventually broken up in 1962 whilst her place in the Duff, Herbert and Mitchell fleet was taken by the German built *Westbay* of 5,579 gross tons which dated from 1936. This same year the 12,349 gross ton tanker

Stanvale was completed in Sweden, and after a short period in service was sold to Danish owners at a considerable profit.

However, the second tanker on order for Billmeir, the *Stancloud* of 12,700 gross tons was duly completed during 1958 by Swan Hunter and Wigham Richardson Ltd., Newcastle, and entered service with the company. In the event this was the last ship built for or ever acquired by Jack Billmeir.

12. THE CLOSING YEARS

In 1959 the Stanhope Steamship Co. Ltd. had the following directors:—
Jack Albert Billmeir, CBE. FICS (Chairman)
Annie Margaret Billmeir
John W. Jones, FCA
Hobart Moore, FCA
   The company secretary was L. F. Lowe, FCCS.

Of the £1,600,000 share capital, the following were the principal shareholders. As can be seen the majority was held by Billmeir himself.

Name	Holding—£
Mrs. Annie Margaret Billmeir, Westbrook, Elstead, Surrey	80,000
Jack Albert Billmeir, Westbrook, Elstead, Surrey	955,180
The Birmingham & District Investment Trust Ltd., Stratton House London, W1	15,000
Box Nominees Ltd., Augustine House, Austin Friars, London, EC2	5,000
Sir Henry C. Brewer, 9, St. Helen's Place, London, EC3	10,500
The British Steamship Investment Trust Ltd., 4b, Frederick's Place, London, EC2	6,000
Robert S. Chipchase, Rose Villa, Harton, South Shields	5,500
Eagle Star Insurance Co. Ltd., 1, Threadneedle Street, London, EC2	6,500
Glyns Nominees Ltd., 67, Lombard Street, London, EC3	5,000
Janne Trustees Ltd and Another, 9, St. Helen's Place, London, EC3	70,000
Lombard Street Nominees Ltd., 3, Change Alley, London, EC 3	20,470
Midland Bank (Overseas) Nominees Ltd., 122, Old Broad Street, London, EC2	7,096
Thos. Stephens and Sons Ltd., 14-20, St. Mary Axe, London, EC3	10,950
Strand Nominees Ltd., 6, Adelaide Street, London, WC2	13,500
J. E. Palmer-Tomkinson, 12, Tokenhouse Yard, London, EC2	5,000

In relation to Duff, Herbert and Mitchell Ltd., the company had the following directors:—
   Jack Albert Billmeir (Chairman)
   Kenneth H. Whitaker
   Leonard F. Lowe
The company secretary was J. H. Bradley.

Of the £40,000 paid up share capital, the following were the principal shareholders:—

Name	Holding—£
Annie Margaret Billmeir, Westbrook, Elstead, Surrey	2,000
Jack Albert Billmeir, Westbrook, Elstead, Surrey	34,000
Kenneth H. Whitaker, Tilford House, Tilford, Surrey	3,000

In the case of the management company — J. A. Billmeir and Co. Ltd., the following were directors:—

Jack Albert Billmeir, CBE, FICS. (Chairman
Annie Margaret Billmeir
Eric R. G. Billmeir
Sir Henry C. Brewer, MBE, FICS.

With Leonard F. Lowe, FCCS., as the company secretary.

Of the £25,000 fully paid up share capital, Billmeir held £20,000 whilst his wife Annie held £5,000. It is interesting to note that Billmeir's brother Eric was also a director of this company, although he did not own shares in any of his brother's ventures.

From 1959 the freight market did not hold firm, and as and when there was even the slightest improvement Billmeir would sell one or more of his ships if the offer was good enough. He gradually reduced the size of his fleet, as the returns did not in any way, in his view, justify the management of such a large number of vessels.

In consequence during 1959 he sold the *Stanpark* (3), *Stanwell* (2), *Stanloch* and *Elstead*. The tanker *Stanloch* was sold for breaking up at Savona, whilst the *Elstead* was traded out to Japan, and then sold for breaking up at Nagasaki. The tanker *Stanpark* (3) returned to the London Greeks who had owned her between 1952 and 1954, but was broken up the following year in Greece, whilst the *Stanwell* (2) spent a further eight years trading before arriving at Kaohsiung for breaking up.

The following year, 1960, saw the disposal of the *Stanrealm*, *Stanbell*, *Stanmore* (7) and *Westbrook*. The *Stanrealm* went to Hong Kong buyers for a further three years' trading before being scrapped at that port in 1963, whilst the ore carrier *Stanbell* survived a further five years before breaking up. The *Stanmore* was broken up at Faslane, where she arrived on May 31 1960, and the *Westbrook* which had been damaged by fire whilst laid up at Barry was sold to John Cashmore Ltd. of Newport where she was towed, for scrapping.

Sad to say, 1961 saw the disposal of a further three ships. Billmeir was a clever man, but during years of poor trading saw little point in owning ships which would trade at a loss. The *Stanfirth* was sold for further trading, and was eventually broken up at Shanghai in 1968, whilst the *Stanthorpe* traded for a further five years before delivery to shipbreakers in Japan. The ore carrier *Stanfield* (2) went to Hong Kong owners as the *August Moon* and was wrecked on September 15, 1966 on the Pratas Reef, in the South China Sea, whilst on a voyage from Calcutta to Yokohama, and became a total loss.

Conditions had not improved by 1962, so that the *Westbay* was sold after a long period laid up at Barry, and arrived at Hamburg on September 2, where the shipbreakers soon demolished her. The following year Billmeir disposed of the last war built ship in the fleet, the *Stanland* (3) which was delivered to breakers at Hong Kong.

Thus in 1963 Jack Billmeir was only trading three ships, however, they were the most modern units, having all been built to his own order. He had come to the decision that in hard times, and the early 1960s did not provide high returns for shipowners, to make a profit of any kind he had to trade modern tonnage. Gone were the days when he had traded a fleet with an average age of twenty-five years. The fleet was now as follows:—

Name	Year Built	Gross Tons
Stancrown	1956	8,002
Stanwear	1956	8,108
Stancloud	1958	12,700 (tanker)

Sadly, on December 22, 1963 Jack Albert Billmeir died. At that time he was only 63 years old, and would in my view have built up the fleet or diversified if he had lived to see any kind of improvement in the freight market.

Incredibly, three days after his death, the *Stancrown,* on Christmas Day, went aground at Klaipeda, while on passage from Halifax with a cargo of wheat. However within a fortnight she had been refloated, but was so badly damaged that she was abandoned to her salvors. Subsequently repaired she traded for a further sixteen years, being broken up at Gadani Beach, Pakistan in 1980.

As a result of Billmeir's death, it was decided to dispose of the business. In consequence, George Nott Industries Ltd., of Market Chambers, Shelton Square, Coventry, who already owned Townsend Car Ferries and P. and A. Campbell Ltd., made an offer which was accepted by the shareholders, of which Jack Billmeir's widow was the biggest. Thereafter the tanker *Stancloud* was quickly resold, trading for a further thirteen years, being broken up at Hong Kong in 1977.

George Nott Industries continued to trade the company and its remaining ship, the *Stanwear,* renaming her in 1966 as the *Lady Era.* However in 1968 she passed to Greek owners, and on February 1, 1977 was wrecked off Port Cartier.

George Nott Industries Ltd., gave way to European Ferries Ltd., and a number of Townsend Thoreson's car ferries were thereafter registered under the ownership of the Stanhope Steamship Co. Ltd. European Ferries themselves have now passed into the control of P. and O. and I doubt if we will see the emergence of the Stanhope Steamship Co. Ltd. again.

Whatever, Jack Albert Billmeir, will always be remembered for being one of the most successful shipowners to be produced in Britain since the First World War. He had a knack of making the best of his opportunities, and I regard him as being responsible for prolonging the Spanish Conflict, which would surely have ended earlier if he had not coordinated the vast quantities of cargo going to and from Republican Spain. He was born with little, but he died a millionaire.

APPENDIX

APPENDIX

FLEET LIST

Name and Period in Fleet	Gross Tons	History
Stanhope (1) 1934-1937	505	1920 built by Gebr. Boot, Leiderdrop, as *Tekelderdiep* for builder's own account; 1920 to E. Noronha-Barros, Portugal, renamed *Estoril;* 1923 to Bulk Oil Steamship Co. Ltd. (J. W. Cook and Co. Ltd.), renamed *London Trader;* 1930 to Tyne-Tees Steam Shipping Co. Ltd., Newcastle, renamed *Sandhill;* 1934 to Stanhope Steamship Co. Ltd. (J. A. Billmeir and Co. Ltd.), renamed *Stanhope;* 1937 to Northern Coasters Ltd. (G. T. Gillie, Blair and Company), Newcastle, renamed *Northern Firth;* 1939 to C. R. Mauritzen, Leith, renamed *Baranda;* 1943 to Barline Transports Ltd. (C. R. Mauritzen), Leith; 1946 to Duff, Herbert and Mitchell Ltd., Salisbury, renamed *Juliet Duff;* 1948 same owners, Cornelis A. Lenson, London, appointed as manager; 1949 same owners, management transferred to Owen T. Williams, Port Dinorwic; 1953 to Dinorwic Slate Quarries Co. Ltd. (Owen T. Williams), Port Dinorwic; 1954 to W. N. Lindsay Ltd., Leith; 1954 broken up by T. W. Ward Ltd., Grays, Essex, on behalf of B.I.S.C.O.
Stanmore (1) 1934-1937	700	1918 built by D. Boot, Alphen a/d Rhin, as *Marsdiep* for Hollandsche Vrachtvaart Maatschapij, Rotterdam; 1919 to Walford Lines Ltd., London, renamed *Jolly Kate;* 1928 to Tyne-Tees Steam Shipping Co. Ltd., Newcastle, renamed *Wooler;* 1934 to Stanhope Steamship Co. Ltd. (J. A. Billmeir and Co. Ltd.), renamed *Stanmore;* 1937 to John S. Monks Ltd., Liverpool, renamed *Stanville;* 21.9.1951 arrived at Preston for breaking up by T. W. Ward Ltd.
Stangrove 1936-1939	516	1895 built by J. L. Thompson and Sons Ltd., Sunderland, as *Skinningrove* for Skinningrove Iron Co. Ltd. (T. C. Hutchinson), Saltburn by Sea; c1920 to John Harrison Ltd., London,

renamed *Hailsham;* 1922 to Skinningrove Iron Co. Ltd. (T. C. Hutchinson), Saltburn by Sea, renamed *Skinningrove;* 1922 to Pease and Partners Ltd., Middlesbrough; 1936 to Stanhope Steamship Co. Ltd. (J. A. Billmeir and Co. Ltd.), renamed *Stangrove;* 6.2.1939 captured by Spanish Nationalist Navy and escorted to Palma, Majorca, cargo — mercury, sulphur, nitrate potash and nitrate ammonia; 23.2.1939 wrecked at Palma in a gale; 1941 raised by Spanish Authorities and placed in the ownership of Francisco and Jose Medina Condeminas, renamed *Castilla del Oro;* 1944 renamed *Condestable;* 1954 to Cia. Naviera Sotileza S. A., Spain, renamed *Sotileza;* 1955 renamed *Mechelin;* 1971 broken up in Spain.

Stanhill (1)   1,236   1900 built by Campbeltown Shipbuilding Co.
1936-1937   Ltd., Campbeltown, as *Eider* for Royal Mail Steam Packet Co. Ltd., London; 1927 to Union Castle Mail Steamship Co. Ltd.; 1936 to Stanhope Steamship Co. Ltd. (J. A. Billmeir and Co. Ltd.), renamed *Stanhill;* 1937 to J. Stavron and Co. Ltd., Greece, renamed *Eider;* 1938 to Adriatico Tirreno Jonis Ligure (A.T.J.L.), S. A., Italy, renamed *Docilitas;* 9.1943 taken over by German Forces; 12.2.1944 sunk at Genoa by Allied air attack; 1947 raised and broken up.

Stanholme (1)   2,473   1927 built by Burntisland Shipbuilding Co. Ltd.,
1936-1939   Burntisland, as *Goleta* for La Tunisienne Steam Navigation Co. Ltd. (F. C. Strick and Co. Ltd.); 1936 to Stanhope Steamship Co. Ltd. (J. A. Billmeir and Co. Ltd.), renamed *Stanholme;* 25.12.1939 mined and sunk off the Bristol Channel with the loss of thirteen crew.

Kenwood   1,374   1912 built by Irvine's Shipbuilding and Dry Dock
1936   Co. Ltd., West Hartlepool, as *New Londoner* for Tyne-Tees Steam Shipping Co. Ltd., Newcastle; 1936 to J. A. Billmeir and Co. Ltd.; 1936 to "Sodeco" Soc. Anon., Panama, renamed *Janu;* 1937 renamed *Cadix;* 1938 captured by Spanish Nationalist Navy off Ceuta; 1940 placed in fleet

of Spanish Government, renamed *Castillo Arevalo;* 1946 to Spanish Navy as a transport; 1960 broken up.

Stancor 1936-1940	790	1904 built by W. Harkess and Son Ltd., Middlesbrough, as *Cherrybrook* for Whiteway and Ball, Teignmouth; 1914 to R. H. Penny and Sons, Shoreham; 1915 renamed *Algardi;* 1924 to Smith, Hogg and Co. Ltd., London, renamed *Alburn;* 1929 to Peacock and Cory (W. S. Peacock), Glasgow; 1931 to E. Bergmann, Talin; 1934 to V. Zatorskis, Riga; 1936 to Stanhope Steamship Co. Ltd. (J. A. Billmeir and Co. Ltd.), renamed *Stancor;* 1937 to V. Zatorskis, Riga (J. A. Billmeir and Co. Ltd.); 1938 to Stanhope Steamship Co. Ltd. (J. A. Billmeir and Co. Ltd.); 5.6.1940 shelled and sunk by German submarine *U48* in position 58.48N, 08.45W.
Stanhope (2) 1937-1950	2,337	1919 built by Caledon Shipbuilding and Engineering Co. Ltd., Dundee, as *War Dagger* for the Shipping Controller; 1919 to Cory Colliers Ltd., London, renamed *Corwen;* 1937 to Stanhope Steamship Co. Ltd. (J. A. Billmeir and Co. Ltd.), renamed *Stanhope;* 1950 to Schulte and Bruns, Germany, renamed *Elise Schulte;* 11.12.1957 arrived at Hamburg for breaking up.
Stanmore (2) 1937	3,222	1920 built by Lloyd Royal Belge (Great Britain) Ltd., Glasgow, as *Asier* for Lloyd Royal Belge, Antwerp; c1935 to Cie. Africaine de Nav. S. A., Belgium, renamed *Mambika;* 1937 to Stanhope Steamship Co. Ltd. (J. A. Billmeir and Co. Ltd.), renamed *Stanmore;* 1937 to Cie. France-Navigation (A. Dunnay), France, renamed *Guilvinec;* 1939 owners in liquidation, Worms and Cie appointed as managers; 19.2.1941 torpedoed and sunk by HMS *Tigress* West of Cap Ferrat.
Stanleigh 1937-1941	1,802	1912 built by G. Seebeck Akt. Ges, Wesermunde, as *Ernst Hugo Stinnes 11* for Hugo Stinnes, Germany; 1920 to Cory Colliers Ltd., London, renamed *Corpath;* 1934 to T. N. Epiphaniades, Piraeus, renamed *Prekla;* 1937 to Stanhope

Name and Period in Fleet	Gross Tons	History

Name and
Period in
Fleet

Gross
Tons

History

Steamship Co. Ltd. (J. A. Billmeir and Co. Ltd.), renamed *Stanleigh;* 14.3.1941 bombed and sunk by German aircraft in the Irish Sea, while on passage from Devonport to Workington in ballast, with the loss of seventeen crew.

Stancrest
1937

462

1920 built by Colby Bros. Ltd., Lowestoft, as *Glanmor* for Glanmor Shipping Co. Ltd. (H. W. Lloyd and F. Wood), Swansea; 1922 to General Steam Navigation Co. Ltd., London, renamed *Sheldrake;* 1937 to Stanhope Steamship Co. Ltd. (J. A. Billmeir and Co. Ltd.), renamed *Stancrest;* 27.2.1937 left London for Bridgwater with a cargo of cement; the following day reported off the Isle of Wight, but nothing further seen or heard of her.

Stancroft
1937-1938

1,407

1908 built by J. Priestman and Co. Ltd., Sunderland, as *Greenbatt* for Newbigin Steam Shipping Co. Ltd., Newcastle; 1937 to Stanhope Steamship Co. Ltd. (J. A. Billmeir and Co. Ltd.), renamed *Stancroft;* 1937 to G. M. Mavroleon, Greece, renamed *Neoptolemos;* 1938 to Stanhope Steamship Co. Ltd. (J. A. Billmeir and Co. Ltd.), renamed *Stancroft;* 27.12.1938 bombed and sunk by Spanish Nationalist aircraft at Barcelona; 19.4.1939 raised by Spanish Authorities and placed in their merchant fleet, renamed *Castillo Almansa;* 1942 transferred to Empresa Nacional Elcano de la Marina Mercante; 1959 to Maritima Colonial y de Comercio S. A., Spain, renamed *Valira;* Later broken up.

Standale
1937

2,456

1908 built by Atel. and Ch. de France, Dunkirk, as *St. Pierre* for Nouvelle Soc. Navale de L'Ouest, France; 1913 owners restyled as Soc. Navale de L'Ouest; 1937 to Stanhope Steamship Co. Ltd. (J. A. Billmeir and Co. Ltd.), renamed *Standale;* 3.4.1937 abandoned by her crew 60 miles North of Leixoes, when her cargo of grain shifted while on passage Antwerp to Cartagena, and subsequently sank.

Name and Period in Fleet	Gross Tons	History
Stanbrook 1937-1939	1,383	1909 built by Tyne Iron Shipbuilding Co. Ltd., Newcastle, as *Lancer* for Fisher Renwick Manchester-London Steamers Ltd.; 1937 to Stanhope Steamship Co. Ltd. (J. A. Billmeir and Co. Ltd.); renamed *Stanbrook;* 1937 to G. M. Mavroleon, Greece, renamed *Polyfloisvios;* 1937 to Stanhope Steamship Co. Ltd. (J. A. Billmeir and Co. Ltd.), renamed *Stanbrook;* 18.11.1939 mined and sunk in the North Sea while on passage Antwerp to the Tyne in ballast, with the loss of her entire crew of twenty-one.
Stancourt (1) 1937	950	1907 built by Clyde Shipbuilding and Engineering Co. Ltd., Glasgow, as *Douglas* for London, Midland and Scottish Railway, Goole; 1937 to Stanhope Steamship Co. Ltd. (J. A. Billmeir and Co. Ltd.), renamed *Stancourt;* 1937 to G. M. Mavroleon, Greece, renamed *Nepheligeretis;* 1938 to B. Athanassiedes (A. Davaris), Greece, renamed *Hermes;* 1938 renamed *Suzy;* 1.1939 damaged by air attack in the Spanish Civil War; 1939 renamed *Ioanna;* 1.6.1940 shelled and sunk by German submarine *U37* 120 miles West of Cape Finisterre while on passage from Alexandria to the Tyne. Crew landed at Vigo.
Stanmore (3) 1937	1,387	1919 built by Forth Shipbuilding and Engineering Co. Ltd., Alloa, as *Morna* for London and Edinburgh Shipping Co. Ltd.; 1937 to Stanhope Steamship Co. Ltd. (J. A. Billmeir and Co. Ltd.), renamed *Stanmore;* 1937 to G. M. Mavroleon, Greece, renamed *Naukratouse;* 1938 to Scotia Corp. (F. Leon), Panama, renamed *Virginia;* 1938 renamed *Patria;* 1938 renamed *Fina;* 1939 to Margit Steamship Co. Inc., Panama; 1941 taken over by the Ministry of War Transport; 1947 to L. R. Schmitt and Company, Denmark; 1950 to Ivers and Arlt, Bremen, renamed *Elisabeth Arlt;* 1959 to General Cement Company, Greece, renamed *Andreas X;* 1964 renamed *Andreas N. Hadjikyriakos;* 1968 broken up in Italy.

Name and
Period in   Gross
Fleet   Tons   History

Name and Period in Fleet	Gross Tons	History
Stanray 1937-1938	880	1904 built by Act. Ges, "Neptun", Rostock, as *Hansa* for Currie's Liverpool and Hamburg Line; 1906 to Union Castle Mail Steamship Co. Ltd.; 1937 to Stanhope Steamship Co. Ltd. (J. A. Billmeir and Co. Ltd.), renamed *Stanray;* 1938 broken up in Belgium.
Stanthorpe (1) 1937-1938	4,524	1915 built by J. Priestman and Co. Ltd., Sunderland, as *Malvern Range* for Neptune Steam Navigation Co. Ltd. (Furness, Withy and Co. Ltd.), Liverpool; 1922 to "K" Steamship Co. Ltd. (Kaye, Son and Co. Ltd.), London, renamed *Kambole;* 1937 to Barry Shipping Co. Ltd. (B. and S. Shipping Ltd.), Cardiff; 1937 to Stanhope Steamship Co. Ltd. (J. A. Billmeir and Co. Ltd.), renamed *Stanthorpe;* 1938 to O. E. Bertin, China, renamed *Yolande Bertin;* 1941 to Panamanian Freighters (Wallem and Company) Panama; renamed *Honduras;* 1946 to Cargueros Panamenos S. A. (Wallem and Company), Panama; 1947 to E-Hsiang Steamship Company, Shanghai, renamed *Foo Hsiang;* 9.11.1953 arrived at Osaka for breaking up.
Stanwold 1937-1941	1,019	1909 built by Osbourne, Graham and Co. Ltd., Sunderland, as Alfred Krelinger for Cie. Belge-Scandinave de Nav. a Vap. Soc. Anon., Belgium; 1916 to Messageries Maritimes Belge S. A., Belgium, renamed *Pervyse;* 1930 to Atkinson and Prickett Ltd., Hull, renamed *Easingwold;* 1937 to Stanhope Steamship Co. Ltd. (J. A. Billmeir and Co. Ltd.), renamed *Stanwold;* 27.2.1941 sank off Brighton, while on passage Newcastle and Southend to Cowes, with the loss of her entire crew of nineteen and two gunners.
Stanwood 1937-1939	4,158	1915 built by Neiherst's Schiffsw, Hamburg, as *Itajahy* for Hamburg Sud Amerika Linie, Hamburg; 1921 to R. P. Houston and Company, Glasgow, renamed *Hesione;* 1937 to Stanhope Steamship Co. Ltd. (J. A. Billmeir and Co. Ltd.), renamed *Stanwood;* 10.12.1939 cargo of coal

Name and Period in Fleet	Gross Tons	History
		caught fire while in Falmouth Roads, and vessel subsequently sank, while on passage Methil to the River Plate.
Sheaf Spear 1937	3,050	1919 built by J. Blumer and Co. Ltd., Sunderland, as *Sheaf Spear* for Sheaf Steam Shipping Co. Ltd., Newcastle; 1937 to Stanhope Steamship Co. Ltd. (J. A. Billmeir and Co. Ltd.); 1937 to Cie. France-Navigation S. A., France, renamed *Bougaron 1;* 1942 seized by the Italian Government and placed in their merchant fleet, renamed *Modena;* 22.3.1943 bombed and sunk by Allied aircraft at Palermo; 1947 salved and broken up at Palermo.
Stanbridge 1937-1939	5,863	1917 built by Richardson, Duck and Co. Ltd., Stockton, as *Beechleaf* for the Admiralty; 1919 to Petroleum "Maats" La Corona, Netherlands, renamed *Limichana;* 1927 to Naphta Industrie und Tanklanlagen A. G. "Nitag", Germany, renamed *Ch. N. Kahan;* 1935 to Europaische Tanklager, Germany; 1937 to Stanhope Steamship Co. Ltd. (J. A. Billmeir and Co. Ltd.), renamed *Stanbridge;* 1939 to Europaische Tankreederei G.m.b.H., Hamburg, renamed *Eurofeld;* Second World War, employed as a Raider supply ship; 24.9.1944 scuttled at St. Nazaire; 1950 raised and broken up.
Stanrock 1937	1,105	1910 built by Earle's Shipbuilding Co. Ltd., Hull, as *Darlington* for Wilsons and North East Railway Shipping Co. Ltd., Hull; 1935 to Ellerman's Wilson Line Ltd., Hull, renamed *Castro;* 1937 to Stanhope Steamship Co. Ltd. (J. A. Billmeir and Co. Ltd.), renamed *Stanrock;* 1937 to E. Godillot (A. Davaris), Panama, renamed *Lydia;* 1938 renamed *Ocu;* 1938 renamed *Ilona;* 1939 to Margit Steamship Co. Inc., Panama, renamed *Sona;* 1940 seized by German forces; 4.1941 bombed and sunk in Adames Bay, Milos Island.
Stancliffe (1) 1937-1938	1,735	1914 built by Blyth Shipbuilding and Dry Dock Co. Ltd., Blyth, as *Aydon* for Aydon Steamship Co. Ltd. (J. Ridley, Son and Tully), Newcastle; 1915 renamed *Jet;* 1917 renamed *Charity;* 1918

renamed *Aydon;* 1920 to Anglo Polish Steamship
Line Ltd. (Leopold Halford (London) Ltd.),
London, renamed *Warszawa;* 1925 to Manor Line
(London) Ltd. (C. Angel and Company, Cardiff),
London, renamed *Brompton Manor;* 1936 to
Drakelow Steamship Co. Ltd., renamed
Drakelow; 1937 to Stanhope Steamship Co. Ltd.
(J. A. Billmeir and Co. Ltd.), renamed *Stancliffe;*
5.1938 lying at Sete in damaged condition; 1938
to P. G. Cottaropoulas, Greece, renamed
Navarinon; 1939 torpedoed by submarine in the
Mediterranean during the Spanish Civil War and
beached in damaged condition; 1939 to Jean
Milonas S. A., Greece renamed *Lena;* 1941 taken
over by the Spanish Government, renamed
Castillo Moncada; 1942 transferred to Empresa
Nacional Elcano de la Marina Mercante, Spain;
16.3.1951 wrecked 2 miles East of Sagres during
thick fog when on voyage from Aguilas to Pasajes
with a cargo of esparto grass.

Stangate   1,289   1912 built by W. Dobson and Co. Ltd.,
1937-1942   Newcastle, as *Elvet* for Sharp Steamship Co. Ltd.
                        (Sharp and Company), Newcastle; 1927 to Manor
                        Line (London) Ltd. (C. Angel and Company,
                        Cardiff), London, renamed *Emsworth Manor;*
                        1936 to Drakelow Steamship Co. Ltd., renamed
                        Drakedene; 1937 to Stanhope Steamship Co. Ltd.
                        (J. A. Billmeir and Co. Ltd.), renamed *Stangate;*
                        7.12.1942 sank off the Wash following a collision
                        with the Greek steamer *Agios Georgious;* while
                        on passage from the Tyne to Portsmouth with a
                        cargo of coal.

Stanfield (1) 2,432 1892 built by Armstrong Mitchell and Co. Ltd.,
1937-1939   Newcastle, as *Cadagua* for Fourcade y Gurtubay,
                        Spain; 1903 transferred to Fourcade y Provot,
                        Spain; 1907 to Rederiakties Banco (Carl J.
                        Banck), Sweden, renamed *Augusta;* 1912 to Lane
                        and Macandrew Ltd., London, renamed
                        Trinidadian; 1913 to Trinidadian Co. Ltd.,
                        Glasgow; 1914 to Gulf Refining Co., USA; 1937

Name and Period in Fleet	Gross Tons	History
		to Stanhope Steamship Co. Ltd. (J. A. Billmeir and Co. Ltd.), renamed *Stanfield;* 1939 broken up.
Stanmount 1937-1941	4,468	1914 built by W. Gray and Co. Ltd., West Hartlepool, as *Ricardo A. Mestres* for Consolidated Goldfields of South Africa Ltd., London, after being launched as *Anerley* for Howard Houlder and Partners Ltd., London; 1914 to Ricardo A. Mestres Ltd. (A. Weir and Company), London; 1919 to Bank Line Ltd. (A. Weir and Company), London, renamed *Wyneric;* 1937 to Stevenson, Hardy and Co. Ltd., London, renamed *Bratton;* 1937 to Stanhope Steamship Co. Ltd. (J. A. Billmeir and Co. Ltd.), renamed *Stanmount;* 24.12.1941 mined and sunk off Yarmouth while on a voyage from London to Grimsby with a cargo of creosote.
Stanforth 1937-1945	1,817	1915 built by Jan Smit Czn., Alblasserdam, as *Dirksland* for Scheepvaart en Steenkolen Maats, Netherlands; 1915 to Stroomv. Maats. Nederlandche Lloyd, Netherlands; 1930 to Shipping and Coal Co. Ltd., London, renamed *Foreland;* 1937 to Stanhope Steamship Co. Ltd. (J. A. Billmeir and Co. Ltd.), renamed *Stanforth;* 17.8.1945 wrecked at Grundkallegrund while on passage Kalix to London with a cargo of timber.
Stanburn (1) 1938-1940	2,881	1924 built by Wood, Skinner and Co. Ltd., Newcastle, as *Hebburn* for Burnett Steamship Co. Ltd., Newcastle; 1934 to Hebburn Steamship Co. Ltd. (W. A. Souter and Company), Newcastle; 1938 to Stanhope Steamship Co. Ltd. (J. A. Billmeir and Co. Ltd.), renamed *Stanburn;* 29.1.1940 bombed and sunk by German aircraft off Flamborough Head, with the loss of twenty-five of her crew.
Stanburgh 1938	1,095	1912 built by Steltiner Oderwerke, Staltin, as *Greif* for Dampfrchiff Geseleschaft Argo, Germany; 1921 to Tyne-Tees Steam Shipping Co. Ltd., Newcastle, renamed *Dunstanburgh;* 1938 to Stanhope Steamship Co. Ltd. (J. A. Billmeir and Co. Ltd.), renamed *Stanburgh;* 4.11.1938

abandoned after an explosion while loading petrol at Sete destined for Spain; 1939 broken up at La Seyne.

Stanhall (1) 1938-1940 — 4,831 — 1932 built by W. Gray and Co. Ltd., West Hartlepool, as *Kepwickhall* for West Hartlepool Steam Navigation Co. Ltd., West Hartlepool; 1938 to Stanhope Steamship Co. Ltd. (J. A. Billmeir and Co. Ltd.), renamed *Stanhall;* 30.5.1940 torpedoed and sunk by the German submarine *U101* in position 48.59N, 05.17W, while homeward bound from Australia to the United Kingdon via Suez with a cargo of sugar. One member of crew lost.

Stanland (1) 1938-1940 — 1,753 — 1912 built by Barclay, Curle and Co. Ltd., Glasgow, as *Borderland* for Liverpool and Hamburg Line; 1919 to Leith, Hull and Hamburg Steam Packet Co. Ltd. (J. Currie and Company), Leith; 1938 to Stanhope Steamship Co. Ltd. (J. A. Billmeir and Co. Ltd.), renamed *Stanland;* 1940 to the Admiralty for use as an ammunition hulk; 1951 broken up at Milford Haven by T. W. Ward Ltd.

Stanwell (1) 1938-1944 — 5,757 — 1914 built by Sir James Laing and Sons Ltd., Sunderland, as *Stockwell* for Well Line Ltd. (Tysack and Branfoot), Newcastle; 1916 to T. and J. Brocklebank Ltd., Liverpool; 1938 to Stanhope Steamship Co. Ltd. (J. A. Billmeir and Co. Ltd.), renamed *Stanwell;* 1944 to the British Government for use as a blockship at the Normandy Beach-head.

Queen of the Bay 1938 — 783 — 1919 built by W. Simons and Co. Ltd., Renfrew, as a Naval vessel, later converted for commercial service and named *Protea;* 1936 to Blackpool Steam Navigation Co. Ltd., Blackpool, renamed *Queen of the Bay;* 1938 to J. A. Billmeir and Co. Ltd.; 1938 to French owners; no other details.

Stanlake 1938-1943 — 1,742 — 1923 built by Swan, Hunter and Wigham Richardson Ltd., Newcastle, as *Marjorie S* for builder's own account with management undertaken by Monkseaton Steamship Co. Ltd., Newcastle; 1923 to Monkseaton Steamship Co.

Ltd., Newcastle; 1926 management placed in hands of E. L. Anderson; 1928 to Cie. des Affreteurs Francais, France, renamed *Courcelles;* 1929 to Constants (London) Ltd. (M. Constant) Cardiff, renamed *Ruckinge;* 1938 to Watts Shipping Co. Ltd. (Watts, Watts and Co. Ltd.), London, renamed *Mortlake;* 1938 to Stanhope Steamship Co. Ltd. (J. A. Billmeir and Co. Ltd.) renamed *Stanlake;* 14.4.1943 torpedoed and sunk by German E-boat 12 miles from Lizard Head.

Stanmore (4)   5,525   1912 built by W. Denny and Bros. Ltd.,
1938-1939   Dumbarton, as *Arracan* for P. Henderson and Co. Ltd., Glasgow; 1938 to Stanhope Steamship Co. Ltd. (J. A. Billmeir and Co. Ltd.), renamed *Stanmore;* 1939 to E. Grounds, Riga, renamed *Everest;* 1940 renamed *Kegums;* 1941 taken over by the United States War Shipping Administration; 1946 returned to E. Grounds, Riga; 1947 wrecked at the entrance to Bordeaux while inward bound from the United States with a Cargo of coal.

Stanfleet   7,951   1920 built by Barclay, Curle and Co. Ltd.,
1938-1939   Glasgow, as *Otaki* for the New Zealand Shipping Co. Ltd., London. (she had originally been laid down as the *War Jupiter* for the Shipping Controller); 1934 to The Clan Line Steamers Ltd. (Cayzer, Irvine and Co. Ltd.), Glasgow, renamed *Clan Robertson;* 1938 to Stanhope Steamship Co. Ltd. (J. A. Billmeir and Co. Ltd.), renamed *Stanfleet;* 1939 to Blue Star Line Ltd., London, renamed *Pacific Star;* 27.10.1942 torpedoed by the German submarine *U509* North West of the Canary Islands, in position 29.15N, 20.57W; 28.10.1942 abandoned by her crew; 30.10.1942 presumed to have sunk; while on a voyage from Rosario via Brazil and Freetown to Liverpool with a cargo of frozen meat and generals.

Stancourt (2)   965   1909 built by Ramage and Fergusan Ltd., Leith,
1938-1939   as *Oder* for Leith, Hull and Hamburg Steam Packet Co. Ltd., (J. Currie and Company), Leith; 1938 to Stanhope Steamship Co. Ltd. (J. A.

Billmeir and Co. Ltd.), renamed *Stancourt;* 1939 to Naviera Ortu-Zara S. A., Panama, renamed *Inaki;* 28.9.1942 bombed and sunk by air attack West of Oporto.

Stangrant 1939-1940 — 5,817 — 1912 built by R. and W. Hawthorn, Leslie and Co. Ltd., Hebburn, as *Port Macquarie* for Port Line Ltd., London; c1924 to William Thomas Shipping Co. Ltd., renamed *Cambrian Marchioness;* 1928 to The Clan Line Steamers Ltd. (Cayzer, Irvine and Co. Ltd.), renamed *Clan Grant;* 1939 to Stanhope Steamship Co. Ltd. (J. A. Billmeir and Co. Ltd.), renamed *Stangrant;* 13.10.1940 torpedoed and sunk by the German submarine *U37* North West of St. Kilda, with the loss of eight crew.

Stancliffe (2) 1940 — 4,511 — 1936 built by Lithgows Ltd., Port Glasgow, as *Dornoch* for Dornoch Shipping Co. Ltd.; 1937 to Primrose Hill Steamship Co. Ltd. (Lambert Bros. Ltd.), London, renamed *Huncliffe;* 1940 to Stanhope Steamship Co. Ltd. (J. A. Billmeir and Co. Ltd.), renamed *Stancliffe;* 12.4.1940 torpedoed and sunk by the German submarine *U37* off the Scottish Coast while on passage Narvik to the United Kingdom with a cargo of iron ore. Twenty two crew lost.

Stanpark (1) 1940-1941 — 5,103 — 1937 built by Sir James Laing and Sons Ltd., Sunderland, as *Haughton Hall* for Chas. G. Dunn Shipping Co. Ltd., Liverpool; 1940 to Stanhope Steamship Co. Ltd. (J. A. Billmeir and Co. Ltd.), renamed *Stanpark;* 19.1.1941 captured by the German battleship *Admiral Scheer* and sunk by gunfire, while on passage from Port Said to the United Kingdom with a cargo of cotton seed.

Stanmore (5) 1940-1943 — 4,970 — 1940 built by W. Pickersgill and Sons Ltd., Sunderland, as *Stanmore* for Stanhope Steamship Co. Ltd. (J. A. Billmeir and Co. Ltd.); 1.10.1943 torpedoed by the German submarine *U223* in position 36.41N, 1.10E, while on passage Middlesbrough to Sicily with a cargo of military stores; ship towed in and beached at Tenes, declared a Constructive Total Loss.

Name and Period in Fleet	Gross Tons	History
Parracombe 1940-1941	4,698	1928 built by W. Gray and Co. Ltd., West Hartlepool, as *Parracombe* for Pyman Bros. Ltd., West Hartlepool; 1940 to Stanhope Steamship Co. Ltd. (J. A. Billmeir and Co. Ltd.); 6.5.1941 bombed and sunk by Italian aircraft 60 miles off Malta, while on passage unescorted from the United Kingdon to Malta, thirty crew lost.
Welcombe 1940-1941	5,122	1930 built by W. Gray and Co. Ltd., West Hartlepool, as *Welcombe* for Pyman Bros. Ltd., West Hartlepool; 1940 to Stanhope Steamship Co. Ltd. (J. A. Billmeir and Co. Ltd.); 4.4.1941 torpedoed and sunk by the German submarine *U98* while on passage from the United States to the United Kingdon with a cargo of grain.
Stanford 1941-1952	5,969	1941 built by W. Pickersgill and Sons Ltd., Sunderland, as *Stanford* for Stanhope Steamship Co. Ltd. (J. A. Billmeir and Co. Ltd.); 1952 to Scindia Steam Navigation Co. Ltd., Bombay, renamed *Jalamohan;* 1961 to Tsavliris (Hellas) Maritime Co. Ltd., (Lebanese flag); renamed *Nigean Star;* 26.2.1962 arrived at Perana, Greece, for breaking up.
Stangarth 1942	5,966	1942 Built by W. Pickersgill and Sons Ltd., Sunderland, as *Stangarth* for Stanhope Steamship Co. Ltd. (J. A. Billmeir and Co. Ltd.); 12.3.1942 torpedoed and sunk by the Italian submarine *Morosini* in position 22.00N, 65.00W, while on passage New York to Table Bay and India on her maiden voyage, with the loss of her entire crew of forty and six gunners.
Stanbank 1942	5,966	1942 built by W. Pickersgill and Sons Ltd., Sunderland, as *Stanbank* for Stanhope Steamship Co. Ltd. (J. A. Billmeir and Co. Ltd.); 5.5.1942 torpedoed and sunk by the German submarine *U103* in position 34.55N, 61,47W (South East of New York), while on her maiden voyage, with the loss of nine crew.

Name and Period in Fleet	Gross Tons	History
Stancleeve 1942-1951	5,970	1942 built by W. Pickersgill and Sons Ltd., Sunderland, as *Stancleeve* for Stanhope Steamship Co. Ltd. (J. A. Billmeir and Co. Ltd.); 1951 to Skibs A/S Preba, Norway, renamed *Akera;* 7.10.1961 arrived at Mirao for breaking up.
Stanhill (2) 1942-1947	5,969	1942 built by W. Pickersgill and Sons Ltd., Sunderland, as *Stanhill* for Stanhope Steamship Co. Ltd. (J. A. Billmeir and Co. Ltd.); 11.5.1947 wrecked off the Ivory Coast, while on passage Lagos to Glasgow with general cargo.
Raby Castle Stanhall (2) 1942-1951	4,996	1925 built by Caledon Shipbuilding and Engineering Co. Ltd., Dundee, as *Raby Castle* for Lancashire Shipping Co. Ltd., Liverpool; 1942 to Stanhope Steamship Co. Ltd. (J. A. Billmeir and Co. Ltd.); 1945 renamed *Stanhall;* 1951 to Wallem and Co. Ltd., Hong Kong, renamed *Ami;* 1956 to Kawasaki Kisen K. K., Japan, renamed *Hisakawa Maru;* 1962 broken up in Japan.
Stanlodge 1943-1952	5,977	1943 built by W. Pickersgill and Sons Ltd., Sunderland, as *Stanlodge* for Stanhope Steamship Co. Ltd. (J. A. Billmeir and Co. Ltd.); 1952 to Bharat Line Ltd., Bombay, renamed *Bharatvijaya;* 1963 broken up at Bombay.
Stanridge 1943-1952	5,975	1943 built by W. Pickersgill and Sons Ltd., Sunderland, as *Stanridge* for Stanhope Steamship Co. Ltd. (J. A. Billmeir and Co. Ltd.); 1952 to Scindia Steam Navigation Co. Ltd., Bombay, renamed *Jalajyoti;* 1965 broken up in India.
Dunkeld Stankeld 1944-1951	4,956	1937 built by Barclay, Curle and Co. Ltd., Glasgow, as *Dunkeld* for Lomond Shipping Co. Ltd. (Robert J. Dunlop), Glasgow; 1944 to Stanhope Steamship Co. Ltd. (J. A. Billmeir and Co. Ltd.); 1945 renamed *Stankeld;* 1951 to Westralian Farmers Transport Ltd., renamed *Swanbrook;* 1957 to John Manners and Co. Ltd., Panama, renamed *Sydney Breeze;* 1964 to San Fernando Steamship Co. S. A., Panama, renamed *San Ernesto;* 1967 to Oriental Trader Navigation Company, Panama, renamed *Cathay Trader;* 1967 to Cathay Trader Steamship Co. Ltd.,

Name and Period in Fleet	Gross Tons	History
		Panama; 1968 to Renown Shipping Corp. S. A., Panama, renamed *Renown Trader;* 8.1.1970 arrived at Hong Kong for breaking up by Cheung Wah.
Stanrealm 1944-1960	7,062	1944 built by Bartram and Sons Ltd., Sunderland, as *Stanrealm* for Stanhope Steamship Co. Ltd. (J. A. Billmeir and Co. Ltd.); 1960 to Liberty Shipping Co. Ltd., Hong Kong, renamed *Fortune Glory;* 27.6.1963 arrived at Hong Kong for breaking up.
Jersey Hart Stanpark (2) 1944-1951	7,275	1943 built by Wm. Doxford and Sons Ltd., Sunderland, as *Jersey Hart* for Morel Ltd., Cardiff; 1944 to Stanhope Steamship Co. Ltd. (J. A. Billmeir and Co. Ltd.); 1945 renamed *Stanpark;* 1951 to T. Dunlop and Sons Ltd., Glasgow, renamed *Queen Eleanor;* 1956 to Douglas Steamship Co. Ltd., Hong Kong, renamed *Inchdouglas;* 14.11.1970 arrived at Kaohsiung for breaking up.
Framlington Court Stancourt (3) 1944-1952	5,026	1924 built by Napier and Miller Ltd., Glasgow, as *Framlington Court* for Court Line Ltd., London; 1944 to Stanhope Steamship Co. Ltd. (J. A. Billmeir and Co. Ltd.); 1945 renamed *Stancourt;* 1952 to Lansdowne and Company, Hong Kong, renamed *Landscape;* 1952 to A. Magsaysay Inc., Philippines, renamed *Ami Banker;* 1955 to Eddie Steamship Co. Ltd., Formosa, renamed *Ally;* 1958 broken up at Keelung.
Stanbell 1945-1960	9,804	1943 built by Sir James Laing and Sons Ltd., Sunderland, as *Empire Beresford* for the Ministry of War Transport, managers — J. A. Billmeir and Co. Ltd.; 1945 to Stanhope Steamship Co. Ltd. (J. A. Billmeir and Co. Ltd.), renamed *Stanbell;* 1955 converted from a tanker into an iron ore carrier, tonnage increased to 10,341 gross; 1960 to Malaya Shipping Co. Ltd. (Pacific Export and Import Co. Ltd.), London, renamed *Kelantan;* 1962 to United Shipping and Investment Co. Ltd.,

Name and Period in Fleet	Gross Tons	History
		London; 1964 to Wilkinson Shipping Co. Ltd., Liberia; 1965 to Phoenix Shipping Co. Inc., Liberia; 1965 broken up at Hirao.
Stanburn (2) 1946	2,767	1919 built by Great Lakes Engineering Works, Ecorse, Michegon, as *Cottonwood* for the United States Shipping Board; 1937 to Soc. Anon. Maritime et Commerciale (B. Burger), Panama, renamed *Adria;* 1939 to Branch Steamship Co. Ltd. (Reginald Jones and Co. Ltd.), Cardiff, renamed *Coity Castle;* 27.11.1944 beached in the River Thames following a collision, and declared a Constructive Total Loss; 1946 sold by Salvage Association to Stanhope Steamship Co. Ltd. (J. A. Billmeir and Co. Ltd.), repaired and renamed *Stanburn;* 27.10.1946 sank after striking a submerged object North of Kerkenah Bank in position 35.15N, 11.55E, while on passage from Algiers to Sfax in ballast.
Stancliffe (3) 1946-1947	2,852	1941 built by W. Gray and Co. Ltd., West Hartlepool, as *Empire Brook* for the Ministry of War Transport; 1946 to Stanhope Steamship Co. Ltd. (J. A. Billmeir and Co. Ltd.), renamed *Stancliffe;* 3.4.1947 abandoned after grounding North West of North Pier, Sharpness Dock, while on passage Emden to Sharpness with a cargo of timber; declared a Constructive Total Loss; wreck sold and taken to Cardiff for repairs; 1948 trading for Newbigin Steamship Co. Ltd., renamed *Gripfast;* 1960 to Saints Anarzyroi S. A., Panama, renamed *Capeton Costas P;* 1966 to Cia. de Nav. Patricio (Liberia) Ltda., Panama, renamed *Karine M;* 1966 to Siconen S. A., Panama, renamed *Pitsa;* 6.12.1967 sank in position 13.32N, 55E, after developing leaks while being towed from Djibouti to Colombo by the salvage tug *Nisos Kerkyra.*
Stanland (2) 1946-1949	4,970	1919 built by American International Shipbuilding Corp., Hog Island, as *Labette* for the United States Shipping Board; 1941 to the Ministry of War Transport, renamed *Empire Ortolan;* 1946 to Stanhope Steamship Co. Ltd. (J. A. Billmeir

Name and Period in Fleet	Gross Tons	History
		and Co. Ltd.), renamed *Stanland;* 1949 to Alma Shipping Co. S. A. (Fares Shipping Co. Ltd.), Panama, renamed *Alma;* 31.3.1953 arrived at Milford Haven for breaking up by T. W. Ward Ltd.
Lexamine 1946-1954	129	1946 built by G. Mulls Engineering Co. Ltd., Plymouth, as Cadet Training ship *Lexamine* for Stanhope Steamship Co. Ltd. (J. A. Billmeir and Co. Ltd.); 1954 to E. Victory, Gibraltar; No other details.
Stanglen *Stanpark* (3) 1946-1952 1954-1959	9,917	1945 built by Sir James Laing and Son Ltd., Sunderland, as *Empire Chancellor* for the Ministry of War Transport; 1946 to Stanhope Steamship Co. Ltd. (J. A. Billmeir and Co. Ltd.), renamed *Stanglen;* 1952 to Tsavliris Shipping Ltd., London, renamed *Newminster;* 1954 to Stanhope Steamship Co. Ltd. (J. A. Billmeir and Co. Ltd.), renamed *Stanpark;* 1959 to Tsavliris Shipping Ltd., London, renamed *Granny Suzanne;* 1960 broken up at Piraeus.
Stanholme (2) 1947	7,674	1945 built by Bethlehem Fairfield Shipyard Inc., Baltimore, as *Sheepshead Bay Victory* for the United States Maritime Commission; 1947 to Stanhope Steamship Co. Ltd. (J. A. Billmeir and Co. Ltd.), renamed *Stanholme;* 1947 to P. and O. Steam Navigation Co. Ltd., London, renamed *Karmala;* 1967 to Mitsui Shipbuilding and Engineering Co. Ltd., Japan, intended for breaking up; 1967 to Nan Tay Industrial Co. Ltd., Kaohsiung for breaking up.
Stanmore (6) 1947	7,675	1945 built by Bethlehem Fairfield Shipyard Inc., Baltimore, as *Mahanoy City Victory* for the United States Maritime Commission; 1947 to Stanhope Steamship Co. Ltd.), (J. A. Billmeir and Co. Ltd.), renamed *Stanmore;* 1947 to P. and O. Steam Navigation Co. Ltd., London, renamed *Khyber;* 1964 to Dragon Steamship Co., Liberia, renamed *Comet Victory;* 1968 to Republic Steamship C. S. A., Liberia, renamed *Ocean Comet;* 21.12.1969 arrived at Kaohsiung for breaking up.

Name and
Period in   Gross
Fleet   Tons   History

Stanthorpe (2) 1947-1949	7,242	1944 built by Bethlehem Fairfield Shipyard Inc., Baltimore, as *Samskern* for the United States Maritime Commission, and on lend/lease to the Ministry of War Transport; 1947 to Stanhope Steamship Co. Ltd. (J. A. Billmeir and Co. Ltd.), renamed *Stanthorpe;* 1949 to Larrinaga Steamship Co. Ltd., Liverpool, renamed *Domingo de Larrinaga;* 1955 to Cia. Nav. Aivali, Liberia, renamed *Vassilis;* 1959 to Cia. de Nav. Guaca, Greece, renamed *Katina;* 1963 to Tarsiano Cia. Nav. S. A., Panama, renamed *Anastassia;* 6.1.1969 went aground off Constanza in heavy weather and abandoned, while on a voyage from Alexandria to Constanza.
Stanmore (7) 1947-1960	10,708	1945 built by Sun Shipbuilding and Dry Dock Co., Chester, Pa., as *Fort Jupiter* for the United States Maritime Commission; 1947 to Stanhope Steamship Co. Ltd. (J. A. Billmeir and Co. Ltd.), renamed *Stanmore;* 31.5.1960 arrived at Faslane for breaking up by Shipbreaking Industries Ltd.
Stanwell (2) 1947-1959	10,722	1945 built by Sun Shipbuilding and Dry Dock Co., Chester, Pa., as *Fort Cheswell* for the United States Maritime Commission; 1947 to Stanhope Steamship Co. Ltd. (J. A. Billmeir and Co. Ltd.), renamed *Stanwell;* 1959 to T. S. Bendizen, Norway, renamed *Landbreeze;* 1960 to Maryland (International) S. A., Liberia, renamed *Panargy 1;* 1963 renamed *Sirod;* 1965 to Cia. Nav. Capistrano S. A., Liberia, renamed *Capistrano;* 7.4.1967 arrived at Kaohsiung for breaking up.
Stanway 1948-1951	2,902	1942 built by W. Gray and Co. Ltd., West Hartlepool, as *Empire Record* for the Ministry of War Transport; 1946 J. A. Billmeir and Co. Ltd. appointed as managers; 1948 to Stanhope Steamship Co. Ltd. (J. A. Billmeir and Co. Ltd.), renamed *Stanway;* 1951 to Comben Longstaff and Co. Ltd., London, renamed *Yorkbrook;* 1954 to Jansens Rederi A/S, Norway, renamed *Elisabeth Jansen;* 1959 to Marine Ventures Corp., Liberia, renamed *Celia B;* 1963 to Prymo Meltemi Cia. Nav. S. A., Liberia, renamed *Saint Mary;* 1964

Name and Period in Fleet	Gross Tons	History
		to Angelmar Shipping Co. Ltd., Liberia, renamed *Sea Maid;* 11.1.1965 arrived at Willemstad in tow with engine damage and found beyond economical repair; 22.6.1966 arrived in tow at Rotterdam for breaking up by Scheepsvaart en Handel Maats.
Stanfirth 1948-1961	7,285	1944 built by J. Readhead and Sons Ltd., South Shields, as HMS *Beauly Firth* for the Royal Navy; 1948 to Stanhope Steamship Co. Ltd. (J. A. Billmeir and Co. Ltd.), converted for commercial service and renamed *Stanfirth;* 1961 to Cia. Nav. y de Comercio Degedo Ltda., Lebanon, renamed *Akamas;* 1966 to Akamas Shipping Co. Ltd., Cyprus; 1968 renamed *Skepsis;* 1968 broken up at Shanghai.
Stanroyal 1948-1952	9,136	1929 built by Deutsche Schiffs-und-Maschinenbau A. G. Vulcan, Hamburg, as *Isar* for Norddeutscher Lloyd., Bremen; 1947 laid up in the River Tyne; 1948 to Stanhope Steamship Co. Ltd. (J. A. Billmeir and Co. Ltd.), renamed *Stanroyal;* 1952 to Hasim C. Mardin, Istanbul, renamed *Haran;* 1959 to Ipar Transport Co. Ltd., Istanbul, renamed *Necip Ipar;* 19.6.1965 arrived at Malic, Turkey for breaking up by Ilhami Soker.
Stanhope (3) 1951-1954	6,034	1951 built by Short Bros. Ltd., Sunderland, as *Stanhope* for Stanhope Steamship Co. Ltd. (J. A. Billmeir and Co. Ltd.); 1954 to U.S.S.R., renamed *Sovetskaya Artika;* No other details.
Stanburn (3) 1951-1954	5,575	1951 built by Burntisland Shipbuilding Co. Ltd., Burntisland, as *Stanburn* for Stanhope Steamship Co. Ltd. (J. A. Billmeir and Co. Ltd.); 1954 to U.S.S.R., converted to a fish carrier with a gross tonnage of 8,211, and renamed *Zapoljarje;* 1979 to George Moundreas, Greece; 12.4.1979 arrived at Karachi for breaking up.
Stanpool 1954	7,347	1954 built by W. Gray and Co. Ltd., West Hartlepool; laid down as *Stanpool* for Stanhope Steamship Co. Ltd. (J. A. Billmeir and Co. Ltd.) but sold while fitting out to U.S.S.R. and completed as *Bogdan Khmelnitsky;* still in service.

Name and Period in Fleet	Gross Tons	History
Westford 1954-1957	7,084	1941 built by Vickers-Armstrong Ltd., Barrow, as *Empire Baxter* for the Ministry of War Transport, managers — Haldin and Philipps Ltd.; 1943 managers changed to Sir William Reardon Smith and Sons Ltd., Cardiff; 1945 to Leeds Shipping Co. Ltd. (Sir William Reardon Smith and Sons Ltd.), Cardiff, renamed *Paris City;* 1954 to Duff, Herbert and Mitchell Ltd. (J. A. Billmeir and Co. Ltd.), renamed *Westford;* 1957 to Cia. Atlantica Pacifica, Liberia, renamed *Severn River;* 1959 to Risa ve Aslan Sadikoglu Komandit Sirketi, Turkey, renamed *Huseyin Kaptan;* 5.12.1962 arrived at Istanbul for breaking up.
Westbrook 1955-1960	8,137	1942 built by Swan, Hunter and Wigham Richardson Ltd., Wallsend, as *Empire Garrick* for the Ministry of War Transport; 1951 to British Oil Shipping Co. Ltd. (Stevenson, Hardy and Co. Ltd.), London, renamed *Alan Evelyn;* 1955 to Duff, Herbert and Mitchell Ltd. (J. A. Billmeir and Co. Ltd.), renamed *Westbrook;* 1960 broken up by J. Cashmore Ltd., Newport.
Elstead 1955-1959	7,061	1943 built by W. Gray and Co. Ltd., West Hartlepool, as *Empire Prowess* for the Ministry of War Transport, managers — J. E. Murrell and Son; 1947 to National Steamship Co. Ltd. (J. and C. Harrison Ltd.), London, renamed *Harperley;* 1955 to J. A. Billmeir and Co. Ltd., renamed *Elstead;* 22.10.1959 arrived at Nagasaki for breaking up.
Stanfield (2) 1955-1961	10,420	1943 built by Sir James Laing and Sons Ltd., Sunderland, as *Thamesfield* for Northern Petroleum Tank Steamship Co. Ltd. (Hunting and Son Ltd.), Newcastle; 1955 to Stanhope Steamship Co. Ltd. (J. A. Billmeir and Co. Ltd.), converted from a tanker to an ore carrier, and renamed *Stanfield;* 1961 to East Sun Shipping Co. Ltd., Hong Kong, renamed *August Moon;* 15.9.1966 wrecked on the Pratas Reef, in the South China Sea, while on voyage from Calcutta to Yokohama, and became a total loss.

86

Name and Period in Fleet	Gross Tons	History
Stanland (3) 1955-1963	7,162	1942 built by Victoria Machinery Depot Co. Ltd., Victoria., B.C., as *Fort Tremblant* for the Dominion of Canada, and bareboat-chartered to the Ministry of War Transport, managers — W. H. Seager and Co. Ltd., Cardiff; 1947 to Tempus Shipping Co. Ltd. (W. H. Seager and Co. Ltd.), Cardiff, renamed *Beatus;* 1955 to Stanhope Steamship Co. Ltd. (J. A. Billmeir and Co. Ltd.), renamed *Stanland;* 1963 broken up at Hong Kong.
Stanloch 1955-1959	9,912	1944 built by Sir James Laing and Sons Ltd., Sunderland, as *Empire Inventor* for the Ministry of War Transport; 1945 to British Oil Shipping Co. Ltd. (Stevenson, Hardy and Co. Ltd.), London, renamed *Vivien Louise;* 1955 to Stanhope Steamship Co. Ltd. (J. A. Billmeir and Co. Ltd.), renamed *Stanloch;* 20.3.1959 arrived at Savona for breaking up by A.R.D.E.M.
Stanthorpe (3) 1955-1961	7,033	1944 built by Shipbuilding Corporation (Tyne Branch), Newcastle, as *Empire Mandarin* for the Ministry of War Transport, managers — Counties Ship Management Co. Ltd.; 1947 to Dorset Steamship Co. Ltd. (Counties Ship Management Co. Ltd.), London, renamed *Lulworth Hill;* 1949 renamed *Castle Hill;* 1949 to London and Overseas Freighters Ltd. (Counties Ship Management Ltd.), London, renamed *London Builder;* 1949-50 converted to oil burning; 1950 to Soc. Armadora Insular S. A., Panama, renamed *Silver Wake;* 1954 to Eastern Seas Steamship Co. Ltd., London, renamed *Navarina;* 1955 to Stanhope Steamship Co. Ltd. (J. A. Billmeir and Co. Ltd.), renamed *Stanthorpe;* 1961 to Mullion and Co. Ltd., Hong Kong, renamed *Ardbrae;* 1.3.1966 arrived at Onomichi for breaking up by Koshin Sangyo K. K.
Stancrown 1956-1964	8,002	1956 built by J. Crown and Sons Ltd., Sunderland, as *Stancrown* for Stanhope Steamship Co. Ltd. (J. A. Billmeir and Co. Ltd.); 25.12.1963 went aground at Klaipeda, while on

passage from Halifax with a cargo of wheat; prior to 10.1.1964 refloated, but was abandoned to salvors; 1964 to A/S Uglands (J. M. Ugland), Grimstad, repaired and renamed *Anette C;* 1965 renamed *Norita;* 1965 to Bulet S. A., Sofia; 1968 to Navigation Maritime Bulgare, Varna, renamed *Smaragd;* 1970 renamed *Philip Totu;* 1978 to Armour Bay Shipping Co. Ltd., Monrovia (Flandermar Shipping Co. S. A., Piraeus), renamed *Anthi Marina;* 1979 to Transway Shipping Corp., Panama (Intermarine Shipping Ltd., London), renamed *Glory Five;* 1980 broken up at Gadani Beach.

Stanwear 1956-1968	8,108	1956 built by W. Pickersgill and Sons Ltd., Sunderland, as *Stanwear* for Stanhope Steamship Co. Ltd. (J. A. Billmeir and Co. Ltd.); 1964 owning company taken over by George Nott Industries Ltd., Coventry; 1966 renamed *Lady Era;* 1968 to Oceanic Freighters Corp., Greece; 1.2.1977 wrecked off Port Cartier in position 50.00N, 66.51W.
Westbay 1957-1962	5,579	1936 built as *Nurnberg* for Norddeutscher Lloyd, Bremen; 5.1945 recovered by the Allies at Copenhagen; 1945 to the Royal Navy as a Depot Ship; 1948 to Irish Bay Lines Ltd. (H. P. Lenaghan and Sons Ltd.), Belfast, renamed *Dundalk Bay;* 1957 to Duff, Herbert and Mitchell Ltd. (J. A. Billmeir and Co. Ltd.), renamed *Westbay;* 2.9.1962 arrived at Hamburg for breaking up by Eisen and Metall A.G.
Stanvale 1957	12,349	1957 built by Uddevallavarvet A/B, Sweden, as *Stanvale* for Stanhope Steamship Co. Ltd. (J. A. Billmeir and Co. Ltd.); 1957 to Rederiet Hermes I/S, Denmark, renamed *Dorothea Basse;* 1962 to Navrom Rouhania Mar., Rumania, renamed *Pace;* 1964 renamed *Prahova;* subsequently broken up.

Name and Period in Fleet	Gross Tons	History
Stancloud 1958-1964	12,700	1958 built by Swan, Hunter and Wigham Richardson Ltd., Newcastle, as *Stancloud* for Stanhope Steamship Co. Ltd. (J. A. Billmeir and Co. Ltd.); 1964 owning company taken over by George Nott Industries Ltd., Coventry; 1964 to Marine Carriers Co. S. A., Panama (Somerset Shipbrokers Ltd., London), renamed *Panos;* 1972 Atlaster Nav. Ltd., Greece, renamed *Evgenia K. Chimples;* 1976 renamed *Aepos;* 1977 broken up at Hong Kong.